CANCELLED

What next?

What next?

Your career-change companion

Kaye Fallick

ALLEN&UNWIN

First published in 2010

Allen & Unwin
83 Alexander Street
Crows Nest NSW 2065
Australia
Phone: (61 2) 8425 0100
Fax: (61 2) 9906 2218
Email: info@allenandunwin.com
Web: www.allenandunwin.com

Cataloguing-in-Publication details are available
from the National Library of Australia
www.librariesaustralia.nla.gov.au

ISBN 978 1 74175 993 8

Set in 9/14 pt Bitstream Cooper Light by Bookhouse, Sydney
Printed and bound in Australia by Griffin Press

10 9 8 7 6 5 4 3 2 1

Mixed Sources

Product group from well-managed
forests, and other controlled sources
www.fsc.org Cert no. SGS-COC-005088
© 1996 Forest Stewardship Council

The paper in this book is FSC certified.
FSC promotes environmentally responsible,
socially beneficial and economically viable
management of the world's forests.

Contents

Tables   ix

Introduction   xi

How to use this book   xv

Acknowledgements   xvii

1   The world of work   1

Why does work matter so much—and what do we need to do to remain employment-relevant? Career paths give way to crazy paving . . . we shift from money to meaning and watch the demise of the full-time job. Remove barriers to find work at any age or stage.

Trevor Barry, stargazer; Hugh Mackay, social commentator; Margaret Goodwin, Canadophile

2   Shift happens   26

Technology has upended the way we work and communicate. The need to understand this is non-negotiable. There are downsides as well as upsides to this massive shift. We are seeing the rise of the nomadic worker, amplified individual and wireless collaboration. It may be all about connectivity anywhere, anytime but strong self management skills are needed.

Graeme Phillipson, research director; David Clarke, Webjet founder; Fiona Coles, HR director; Alison Armstrong, web entrepreneur

3   What makes you tick?   48

Do your core values match the work you do? Or is there a fundamental disconnect between what matters to you most and the way you earn your income? How can you understand your own personality— and work out which life skills are the most satisfying? What career transition assistance is there to be had from books and the internet— or should you seek the services of a career development professional?

Susie Farmer, receptionist; Jimmy Pham, humanitarian; Linda White, Italophile and travel agent; Dr Peter Carey, career development practitioner

4   Your work DNA   74

Your qualifications, skills, experience and achievements set you apart from the rest. Define your career anchors and business interests to find new directions. Where and how do you really want to work: city, country, office or home? Are you a lone ranger or team player? Using a SWOT analysis will help you in your 'business of one'.

Lisa Shergold, Bus driver; Peter Hatherley, teacher and actor; Professor Barbara Pocock, work-life balance researcher and academic

5   What's out there?   101

How do you reinvent yourself to make the most of the new project-based work opportunities? What sorts of projects are available? Which are the fastest growing employment sectors? And is it possible to move from an emphasis on money to more meaningful employment? How do you find your special cause, become a volunteer or take time out to rethink and reflect upon the best way forward?

Phil Ruthven, futurist; Tim Spurdens, volunteer; Donny Morrison, English language teacher

6   Planning your next move   128

Move beyond the theory of career change and into action. Learn to let go of the past and consider future options. Radical change versus gentle career segue—which one's for you? Use the scorecard to evaluate your next move. Commit to a new path, set goals and deadlines. Or consider re-negotiating your current role to better suit your personal life.

Ella James, entertainer; Catherine Lockhart, life coach; Jen Bird, tour operator

7 Selling your talents 154

Secure the work you really want. How do people get hired? How will you add value in your next role? Read about three very different approaches to finding work. Do the necessary research and meet the right people via an informational interview. Create a robust resume, open the right doors and handle yourself with confidence in an interview.

Alan Maxwell, IT consultant and tour operator; Fiona Corr, mature-age PhD student; Hugh Davies, career transition director

8 Skilling up 181

Stay ahead of the pack by investing in professional development for your business of one. Evaluate your skills, attributes and capabilities. It's not what you have, but how you use it. Understand the five categories of skills and how you need to maintain them to stay relevant.

Gary Henderson, career transition consultant; Doreen Spurdens, volunteer teacher; Les Bartlett, baker

9 Be your own boss 200

Do you have what it takes to run your own business—and will it be a small, medium or large enterprise? A start-up or something you buy into? Who is your potential customer—by age, location or need? How can you learn more about your market? Are you a born entrepreneur or an able technician? Whichever you are, have you got the five essential ingredients for business success; personality, passion, persistence, plan and (deep) pockets?

Natasha Boyd, bookseller; Professor John English, author and academic; Tim Terry, truffle farmer; Hugh Evans, former franchisee

10 New tricks 223

Ageism has long been a fact of life for many mature workers. But as retirement is redefined as a time of new purpose, priorities, careers and opportunities, the concept of a use-by date is fast disappearing. The need for skilled and experienced staff means older men and women can head towards the work they want—not the work they have had to do. But mature workers will need to stay connected, skilled and abreast of new ways of working in order to remain employment-relevant.

Tim Lane, broadcaster and writer; Phil Ruthven, futurist; Leonard Cohen, singer and songwriter; Elizabeth Broderick, Commissioner responsible for Age Discrimination; Connie Vallis, computer whiz

11   Your time starts now   **245**
Old ways of working are disappearing and freedom, independence, flexibility and work-life balance are more than achievable. You can influence the pace and nature of your career transition. Use this ten-point program to start your change now.

Notes and Resources   254

Tables

1.1	Connecting your career dots	22
1.2	Trevor's career dots	24
3.1	Just luck? Or within your locus of control?	52
3.2	Defining success	56
3.3	Your values	61
3.4	What excites you?	66
3.5	Your favourite life skills	68
4.1	Educational qualifications	79
4.2	Auditing your skills	80
4.3	Projects achieved	84
4.4	Defining your career anchors	88
4.5	Defining your business interests	90
4.6	Working environments	95
4.7	Your career SWOT analysis	97
5.1	Australian jobs 2008	118
5.2	Australian jobs 2008—predicted growth	120
6.1	Competing career paths	141
6.2	Goal-setting	145
6.3	Removing obstacles	150
7.1	Finding work	158
8.1	Your skills	196
9.1	Buying a franchise	214
9.2	Your business success	217

Introduction

Do you feel captive to poor career decisions made by your teenage self?

Tethered to the desk, the factory, or the office?

Trapped in a career that lacks fun and a sense of purpose?

You know there's a party going on somewhere in the workplace, but you haven't received the invitation and don't know the directions?

You're not alone.

What Next? is written for anyone who is considering their career options, questioning their current role—or, perhaps, forced into unemployment or redundancy well before their time. It's also for those who 'quite like' the work they do, but feel there is something missing in their working lives, something else they could do which would bring more meaning and satisfaction.

There has been a dramatic increase in flexibility in the workplace over the past 30 years but the positive side of these developments is rarely reported in Australia. My role as a magazine and website publisher, and a director at large of the International Federation on Ageing (IFA) gives me access to the latest international thinking on work and how we can all remain employment-relevant.

One conference, in particular, titled Reinventing Retirement and held in Singapore in January 2009, featured speaker after speaker who predicted positive options and ongoing engagement for experienced workers in developed nations in the years to come—as long as they used the flexibility now available within the workplace to remain skilled and connected.

This positive message has been either missed or misunderstood by the media in Australia. Instead, reports about work seem to have concentrated on the negatives of the work experience; long hours, stress, rising unemployment and poor work environments. Such lack of balance convinced me there was a critical need for a plain-English guide which explained changes occurring in the way we work, with an emphasis on the many positive strategies we can all adopt to rejuvenate our working lives on our own terms—whether as paid employees, contractors, consultants or in micro, medium or massive business startups.

The increasing feminisation and casualisation of the workforce, the death of the 'day job' and the revolution in technology-driven communication have dramatically expanded our work options. But the new workplace 'rules of engagement' call for an equally dramatic rethink of our working selves, what we have to offer, and new approaches to a job search, career change or business startup.

No longer can we get a 'job' then rest content, happily pigeonholed as a nurse, or gardener or accountant. It is much more likely that, rather than being offered a full-time salaried position, we will now be awarded a project or short-term contract; provided, of course, that our skills match those required. This places the onus fairly and squarely back on us to continually upgrade our skills and maintain our professional development.

The following chapters offer a step-by-step guide to remaining fit for the workplace today—and tomorrow. We readily understand the need for regular physical and mental exercise to maintain a healthy body and mind. Our work-fitness routine must be viewed in the same way. The employment market is becoming increasingly complex and evermore challenging, but it also has the potential to be even more rewarding. We just need to be fit to tackle it.

We now need to consider ourselves as a 'business of one' with a tool kit of relevant skills, experience, aptitudes and achievements which keeps us ready and able to supply services on an as-needed basis. These services may be delivered within traditional full-time employment, but are increasingly likely to involve a pay-per-performance model.

Complementing the shift in the way we work and how we are hired is a movement slowly gathering force around the world, driven by people who are questioning a workplace reward system based on status or money. These workers, instead, wish to be rewarded by the impact they have made on community service, environmental goals or political causes. This shift from money to meaning involves people of all ages and stages who have decided their work must allow them to leave a positive legacy, but it is particularly prevalent amongst more mature workers who are refusing to don the slippers of retirement and publicly confirm they have reached their use-by date.

Their career credo is that there doesn't necessarily have to be a disconnect between having an impact and earning an income. And that we shouldn't think we have to wait until we have 'made it' on other people's terms before we do the work which rewards our souls.

What Next? synthesises expert opinion on these significant work trends and offers you the strategies to rethink the how, why, when and where of your own working life. It does this in four main ways:

- by explaining the dramatic changes that have occurred in the workplace during the past 50 years and how they will affect your particular work future
- by encouraging you to take a step-by-step approach to exploring your work motivations and your 'work DNA' and to understand how this information can form the basis for positive career decisions
- by sharing insights from career transition professionals and social commentators on the best way to stay actively engaged in productive work
- by explaining how you can best review your own career to date, and create a plan, based on the 'Connecting the career dots' grid

of six potential areas of change—sector, organisation, role, work arrangement, location and education—to move more smoothly toward a role that satisfies. The career dots grid can be used time and again when you feel your career path is veering out of control . . . or during an annual review of your assets and your opinions.

You will meet many people in the pages of this book: people like Les, who made the segue from banker to baker with a stint of taxi-driving in between. Or Margaret, who made her lifelong dream of living in Canada come true after a 'false start' as a film editor. People like Trevor, whose incredible change from mine mechanic to astronomer was reinforced by distance education, and David, whose drive to deliver a better travel booking system led to the formation of Webjet.

These very different but equally successful career changers can provide inspiration and encouragement to help you decide not to settle for second best in *your* career, but to tailor a really exciting 'business of one' as they have.

You'll have to do some work, of course—there is still no free lunch. So be prepared to devote some serious thinking time as well as make a committment to work through the exercises and fill in the tables. Your reward will be clear insights and useful strategies for a more satisfying work life.

Let's recap the good news:

- As our work futures have become less secure, so our opportunities to enjoy many interesting work assignments, as opposed to one job per life, have increased dramatically.
- The 'death of the day job' has the potential to liberate everyone. Some may view the increased casualisation of the workforce as a reduction in workers' rights and security. Conversely, it can be seen as an opportunity to tailor the job you want to fit your life.
- An increasingly flexible workplace and fresh ways of thinking can lead to new types of work performed in new locations at

more convenient times—as long as we know our rights and are prepared to hang tough in our negotiations.

- We are moving towards a time of increased meritocracy in the workplace, when the best man or woman for the job, rather than the most senior, the most feared, or the most influential, may well be the one who is hired.

- Most importantly, we are also moving to a time when, largely due to technology, we have far more control over our own work destinies, particularly in our ability to access affordable education and training as, when and where we need it.

This means that whatever you've done before no longer needs to be a guide to what comes next.

Exciting?

Very!

Scary?

Just a little.

What Next? will address your fears and reinforce the positives for your future work. So open your mind and your heart to your own very real possibilities. Pick up a pen and take a few short hours to see how these changes and this book can help you connect your career dots in a truly exciting way.

How to use this book

This book is not intended to be read once and then put aside. As its title suggests, it is a companion whose advice, support and resources are there to be accessed on an 'as needs' basis. You may feel in need of a holistic view of your work options and opportunities, so a first reading could mean skimming chapters 1 to 11 in their entirety. Or you may have a pressing need to impress a prospective client, so you'll just read Chapter 7, Selling Your Talents. Or a burning desire to start your own small business, in which case Chapter 9, Be Your Own Boss, will help.

However you first approach *What Next?* it will hopefully provide a strong sounding-board for your career transitions today, tomorrow and beyond.

Whichever order you choose, make sure you understand the process of career change explained in Chapter 1, in particular the six-step 'Connect your career dots' grid. This grid has been created to give you a blank table to fill in as you need it. It is also downloadable from <www.what-next.com.au> and can be used whenever you need to cut through career confusion and help prioritise the next most useful steps.

Acknowledgements

While works of fiction may be exclusively the product of a singular and brilliant imagination, little worthwhile non-fiction has been written by a single human being.

Non-fiction is overtly, or covertly, a much more collaborative exercise: overt when the author interviews or researches the ideas of others; covert when we absorb wisdom or experiences of others and weave it in with our own words.

So this is a thank you to the many people whose brains I have picked, those who agreed to be interviewed and share, in many cases, a lifetime of intellectual property, or emotionally painful journeys, or adversity, or reversals in fortune as well as their achievements and joy. In most cases the subject of the interview did not know me when I made the cold call to ask if they would tell me about their work-life experiences.

The resulting interviews are presented in two different ways—either as 'real person' profiles to help illustrate how others have fought the good fight in the workplace to achieve a role which does indeed make them bound out of bed in the morning or as a 'ask the expert' comment when the view of an expert with long-term experience casts light on an aspect of career change and management.

So a very sincere thank you to all the following interviewees whose personal stories, insights and anecdotes form the backbone of this book:

Trevor Barry

Hugh Mackay

Margaret Goodwin

Graeme Phillipson

David Clarke

Fiona Coles

Alison Armstrong

Susie Farmer

Jimmy Pham

Linda White

Dr Peter Carey

Lisa Shergold

Peter Hatherley

Professor Barbara Pocock

Phil Ruthven

Tim Spurdens

Donny Morrison

Ella James

Catherine Lockhart

Jen Bird

Alan Maxwell

Fiona Corr

Hugh Davies

Gary Henderson

Doreen Spurdens

Les Bartlett

Natasha Boyd

Professor John English

Tim Terry

Hugh Evans

Tim Lane

Phil Ruthven

Leonard Cohen

Elizabeth Broderick

Connie Vallis

Authors often believe they are the prime agents in the creation of a book. They are not. So my warmest thanks to Andrea McNamara who had the faith to back this concept, to my publisher, Sue Hines, for her insight and ongoing support, to editor Ann Lennox for her professional and intelligent shaping of the manuscript, copy editor Karen Ward for her many improvements and proofreader *par excellence* Karen Tait whose suggestions were the icing on the cake.

Gary Henderson is a dear friend who deserves a special mention. A genuine expert in career transition, he has forgotten more than I could ever hope to learn about the place of work in our lives and has shared this knowledge generously.

Chris Harrington and Deborah Holland from Books in Print have also offered ongoing support and intelligent feedback on what a book about work might offer.

Every writer might need a room of their own but Geraldine and John McGrath upped the ante magnificently by offering me unlimited access to Cottontree—a house of my own—to start my research and thinking.

This book could not have been completed without the support of my work colleagues in our real and virtual office—in particular Debbie McTaggart, Drew Patchell, Ellie Hilton, Helen Jackson, Pamela Oddy and Rob Kirk—who picked up the slack when I went missing in action to write, and offered support, ideas and contacts when questions arose. Similar thanks are owed to Susie and Norman at Oskar Whyte who kept up a steady flow of excellent coffee as I toiled.

And last, but never least, I thank my gloriously dysfunctional, warm and supportive family. Lucy who never failed to send messages of support by text and email from Argentina, SJ whose practical business sense far exceeds her youth, and Davy who read every word—at least twice—sharing feedback, correcting grammatical glitches, and debating, late into the night, the fine art of placing a comma.

1

The world of work

Nearly 60 per cent of Australian workers work five days a week with a further 18 per cent working six or seven. This amount of time represents the majority of their waking hours: more time spent at the workplace than with family, friends, spouse or partner; more time than relaxing or pursuing a favourite hobby. That fact alone should encourage us to make sure the hours we work are both enjoyable and meaningful. The old concept of work as a chore to be endured is being increasingly challenged, as is the notion of a lifetime of service rewarded by a leisure-filled retirement. Now workers of all ages are wishing to perform meaningful tasks. The good news is that the changes occurring in the workplace—in particular those wrought by technology and an increase in female participation in the workforce—have delivered much more flexibility in work arrangements and options.

This chapter explains these changes and how they can help you revise your work arrangements towards a more meaningful role. It also introduces the concept of Connecting your career dots to help you identify ways of approaching career change.

Imagine this

You sleep deeply for eight hours and wake naturally at 6.30 am, swing your legs over the side of the bed ready to go for your regular early morning walk, jog, or gym session.

Getting back home at 7.30 am means time for a shower, breakfast and a quick skim of the morning newspapers before heading to work.

Your mood is anticipatory. Already, under the shower, you have had a multitude of ideas about how to spend the day, use your time effectively and rise to the challenges of the work you do.

Some of these challenges are ongoing. Some are short-term issues or concerns that need addressing sooner rather than later.

None bother you too much.

You love what you do, and have faith in your ability to negotiate your way through whatever your working life throws at you. You also enjoy the interaction with colleagues you respect and the ongoing opportunities for training and personal development.

You are in a role you love, doing worthwhile work for a fair remuneration.

Congratulations.

You have connected *your* career dots and will remain engaged, enthusiastic and work-relevant—no matter what your age or stage.

Sigh

The alarm has gone off and the dream is over. You drag yourself out of bed—no time to walk or exercise—grunt at the family or the dog or cat, throw down a bowl of muesli and wander, reluctantly, out the front door to do the same thing you've done for far too long, for too little praise and too little money. You feel stuck, mid-career, mid-life, mid-everything.

You're right. You are stuck and can't see a way forward.

But who says you have to remain stuck for the rest of your life?

Trevor Barry:
Stargazer

profile

'At no stage should anyone ever look at something they want to do and say, "I can't do that".'

So says Trevor Barry, who has just worked from 9.30 pm until 3.30 am. Rather than feeling tired, he's elated by what he's been doing—viewing a lineup of no fewer than four moons around Saturn. In fact this sense of wonder and excitement pervades just about everything he says. An interesting phenomenon for a miner who retired at 52 with debilitating injuries and a fear of the future, mainly because he had no clue what he would do or if he would ever work again.

Born and educated in Broken Hill, Trevor left school at sixteen. He needed a job and the only job in town was as an apprentice fitter and machinist at the mine. During the following three decades Trevor worked all over the mine sites and retrained twice—first as a refrigeration engineer, then as an electrician. Each time the new qualification was recognised with a wage rise, Trevor put the increase straight into superannuation. So in 2002 when he knew he would be retrenched due to the closure of the mine, money wasn't his first concern. His major issues, instead, were what he would do next and his health.

'It was scary—the first time in my life with no job. I also pictured myself in a wheelchair when I was told how severe my back problems were. It wasn't so much what I wanted to do, but more about what I could do.'

Happily Trevor had a hobby which had grown into an over-whelming passion—astronomy. Some fifteen years earlier, a younger apprentice, Steve, asked Trevor if he would like to see the telescope Steve and his dad, Geoffrey, had built.

'I had no interest in the night sky but I went along for a look. I could see a lot of fuzzy patches—and learned they were galaxies. It knocked my socks off. It was as though someone had lifted a veil. I went home determined to make my own telescope and learn more about astronomy.'

Fast forward to 2002 and Trevor's retrenchment. He applied for a degree in Science (Astronomy) at Swinburne University as a distance learner. His years as an amateur astronomer, and the strong support of recognised stargazers, helped him overcome the need for prior educational qualifications but he was required to achieve a minimum of credit passes in all subjects, throughout the degree. His passion and determination to learn resulted in high distinctions in all subjects and the faculty's Award for Excellence in September 2005 as the top graduating student.

Trevor has now built his own observatory at the bottom of his garden and hosts many visits for school groups and other interested stargazers. His work has been recognised by NASA via the Cassini RPWS (Radio & Plasma Wave Science) team and he was recently invited on a study trip to the W.M. Keck Observatory in Hawaii with a professional research team from Swinburne.

Money is still not a major incentive for Trevor. He has chosen to share his research and knowledge for free.

'Why would I charge?' he asks. 'I don't think of this as work.'

Trevor Barry is a former miner and passionate amateur astrologer

Work matters

Work matters for many reasons.

It matters, most obviously, as a way of earning a living, paying bills, putting food on the table, and groceries in the pantry.

But it matters for many other, equally compelling reasons.

Work matters because humans were not created to be idle. When they are idle trouble brews, whether in the Garden of Eden or a block of flats in the inner suburbs.

Lack of work is a problem not just because we will get into mischief (which is highly likely) but more because we will almost certainly feel bad about ourselves. It will be that much harder to get out of bed the next day; we become a little more slothful and so feel a little slower, a little less vital. We will begin to fall apart.

'Things fall apart, the centre cannot hold' wrote Irish poet, W.B. Yeats, in 1920. Yeats was speaking metaphysically more than a century ago, describing the sense of confusion in post-war Europe. But this sense of turmoil also applies to the rapid pace of change in the workforce. Yet, for most people in the twenty-first century, work can also offer a sense of purpose, a timetable, an order and structure in our daily lives. It can allow us to enjoy a meaningful engagement with the wider world.

Something to do

Someone once said that the ingredients of a happy life are having someone to love, something to do and something to look forward to.

This book is about finding something to do—something that is personally satisfying, has meaning for you and others, and is financially rewarding.

Generally speaking, regardless of fluctuations in the world's economies, there is a growing shortage of labour, the ramifications of which will be felt, over the next five to ten to twenty years, in just about every corner of the globe. This is the macro situation—there will be more jobs than workers to fill them. So theoretically, there will be no reason why you cannot get work, whatever your age or stage.

But reality indicates that there is no reason for complacency. The world of work has changed dramatically over the past twenty years, as it will continue to change over the next twenty. However, in order to fully benefit from the new landscape of work, we should recognise and act upon two important factors.

First, we need to recognise that the responsibility for our work future and employment relevance lies squarely upon our own shoulders. The conditions are changing in favour of job seekers, but regardless of what happens at a macro level, only *you* can increase your own personal chances of finding satisfying work. Second, we will need to gain an understanding of the dynamics of the world of work and commit to becoming more adaptable, or 'change ready'. This involves an acceptance of the way the workplace has changed rather than yearning for an older, more stable work landscape.

Putting the runners on

One of the simplest and most effective ways of adapting to change is to understand the lesson offered by Dr Spencer Johnson in his bestselling book *Who Moved my Cheese?* This modern-day parable on change tells the story of two mice who are enjoying a predictable existence until one day their plentiful supply of cheese runs out. What to do? Initially their reactions are similar; they are shocked, disappointed and angry. They bemoan their bad luck and mourn the loss of the cheese. Then their attitudes diverge. Hem continues to mourn the loss of the cheese and the unfairness of life in general. Haw puts on a pair of runners and learns to navigate his way out of the maze in which he and Hem are imprisoned. He gets moving. In fact, he starts running. And by doing so he locates another store of cheese—a far larger amount, as it happens.

Hem has discovered the secret to change. When change is thrust upon us, we need to change ourselves. Sooner or later we need to stop grieving for what has passed, learn new skills and take new actions to gain what can still be had.

Is this where you are, in career terms, right now? Stuck in a maze where the supply of cheese (job satisfaction, income, professional development, or all three) has disappeared?

The sad fact about career change is that very few of us are ready when it occurs. This change may come as a shock, in the form of retrenchment, or as a gradual dwindling in job satisfaction when you find yourself simply doing the same tasks over and over. Or perhaps your own personal priorities, goals or values have shifted. You could be a new parent, or recently bereaved, or less energetic or physically able than you once were and the importance of your work no longer stands up under scrutiny.

Whatever the reason, the need for a career change, intellectually, is usually experienced far in advance of the emotional acceptance of this need. So if you are indeed feeling lost in the maze, console yourself with the fact that this is a normal reaction. The good news is that there are many useful and effective strategies to get unstuck and move ahead.

The first priority is to more fully understand the context of the world of work, and how it functions today.

What is work?

Some people love what they do so much they would do it for no salary. Usually these are the very people who can command high salaries and enjoy strong public recognition. People such as Rove McManus, Dr Fiona Wood, and Dr Tim Flannery are examples. Others loathe what they do and live for Friday evening when they can escape the workplace and head straight to a local watering hole in order to feel better about themselves. This is the other end of the scale and it's likely these workers don't command a particularly high salary in return for their clock-watching approach. The rest of us are probably somewhere in between.

The earliest form of work was indistinguishable from survival. The stronger of the species (usually male) went out of the cave to kill beasts for supper. Childbearing women looked after the offspring, prepared the 'kill' for consumption, gathered berries and organised basic clothing or shelter. Things changed when nomadic people started to settle and cultivate crops. Homemaking, weaving and crop management became more important. Still later the advent of writing and printing and the creation of simple tools and machinery meant further work specialisation. Human communication and interaction in the form of politics, theatre and sport also increased the diversity of careers such as courtiers, soldiers, actors and jousters. The arrival of the Industrial Revolution forced those who had previously worked on the land or in their own homes into factories and down mines. Armies of peasants became factory fodder. During the twentieth century a new band of workers started to appear in the service industries; those whom organisational expert Peter Drucker termed 'knowledge' workers because they were paid for their brain power and not their physical skills or strength. Initially, knowledge workers also gathered in local 'factories' (offices), often working in open-plan environments with tens, hundreds or thousands of colleagues.

Specialisation

Jobs continued to become more specialised. Consider the human resources industry as an example. First there were managers who looked after other managers. Then human resource experts, and those who studied human resources, those who wrote about the human resource contribution, those who managed how all those employees would be paid, those who took care of the ergonomic aspects of the job, those who coordinated their vehicle leases, those who counted how much tax they would pay, those who designated what they should wear, those who designed their briefcases, or computers, or computer software, or staff rosters. You get the idea.

Computers make it complicated

With the 1960s came the creation of the first mainframe computer—a knowledge working machine. Basic functions such as mathematical calculations, word processing and data manipulation could now be accurately achieved in minutes if not seconds, a change that had an immediate impact on secretarial, clerical and administrative jobs. In 1969 the internet was 'born' in a room in Menlo Park, California and the sharing of knowledge now occurred by cable connection. Within a few years even cable is likely to become obsolete, with work teams sharing ideas and information via wireless—or through thin air, so to speak. The need for the majority of a company's workers to gather daily in one place, at one time, has suddenly and literally disappeared.

Many workers are now (technically at least) free to go where they want and work when they want as long as they deliver.

But this notion of 'distance' work can be strangely unsettling.

And no wonder. Because work, for most people, has never been just about the work they complete. It is also heavily predicated on the social environment, the sense of connection, and the sharing of ideas, energy and trust with other human beings in real time and space.

A perpetual holiday is a good working definition of hell.
—George Bernard Shaw

Hugh Mackay
Why work matters

Work is a potent symbol for both men and women. If we are working it means we are not 'finished'. This is particularly true for the Baby Boomer generation.

There are many reasons why work matters:

- Work provides a stimulating human setting and gives us a herd to connect with, a tribe, or organisation.
- There is gratification associated with completion of tasks which delivers an enormous sense of satisfaction.
- Most work is paid. This is a tangible sign you are valued and will be rewarded.

There is little point in trying to rank these factors, as all three bring real satisfaction to the thing called work. Status may also matter, but is less important than the other three. For the vast majority of people it is not so much about where they are on the ladder.

We are definitely seeing a shift in work from money to meaning. People are saying, 'There's more to life than this treadmill.' But there

---

is no one trend for jobs of the future; there are many trends, some of which are contradictory. For instance, will we work from home or not? Yes is the answer—we will and we won't. The people who will thrive, listen carefully to young people. They are our signposts. This generation of kids will show us how to work. I don't think older people have realised the rate at which we need to update.

Hugh Mackay is a social forecaster and author

Other benefits of work include:

- an opportunity for meaningful engagement—human beings, it seems, can only cope with so much 'play' before they get bored
- ongoing learning or professional development—an aspect many employees regard as more valuable than a pay increase
- sense of purpose—similar to engagement, but more a sense of doing something both useful and beneficial to others
- interactions with peers of different backgrounds or age groups

The new workplace?

Over the millennia there has been a dramatic shift in the notion of 'work'—from the successful spearing of a wild boar, to the successful upload of a graphic file or the successful care of a demented elder. All of these activities constitute work. We accept that the content of the work we perform has changed. But how do we make sense of the rapid pace of change in the workforce in terms of our own careers? What do we need to understand in order to shape our future directions?

First, it is important to move beyond confusion about the many options now available in the world of work. The old adage that too much choice just leads to no choice is very true. Instead, it is preferable to see this plethora of options as a real advantage in a job search. If all bets are indeed off as to where and when you might work, then you can much more easily negotiate a position to best suit your particular availability.

Many workplace changes are directly linked to new technological capabilities. This means some jobs are disappearing, whilst others are being created. One such example is the effect of the facsimile (fax) machine. Before the use of the fax machine became common in the mid-1970s, legal offices would employ 'runners' to deliver original documents to the relevant parties. In recent years the recognition of a fax as a legal document has been accepted and this new, far less expensive method of transmitting documents has quickly replaced the need for a runner. This is but one tiny example of tasks and jobs that have been replaced by technology in recent decades.

From career paths to crazy paving

It used to seem so much easier—if a touch restrictive. First you attended primary and secondary school, leaving secondary in your late teens. The less academic or engaged students left early (from fifteen onwards) and often worked in the trades, retail sector or factories. The more academically inclined often continued into tertiary education, either in a technical environment, or to university, graduating after three or more years with a diploma or degree. A handful undertook postgraduate degrees, but most commenced work. Work for women was often interrupted by childbearing and raising, but for men it usually meant a 40-year stretch, punctuated by annual leave or time off if they changed jobs. Many workers remained in the same industry all their working lives. In their late fifties or early sixties they would retire and often not engage in meaningful work again before dying, within ten or twenty years. If this sounds very boring, soul-destroying and predictable, that's because it probably is. And because our own expectations for later life are now much more robust and exciting.

Most people's ability to learn, work or take a sabbatical was directly connected to their age and life stage. If they were young, society understood they were in a 'learning' phase. Those aged in their mid-twenties and older were expected to remain in paid employment (mothers excepted) until they had reached their use-by date—retirement age—and then they were expected to fade quietly into the sunset, no longer able to contribute.

Happily, these days have gone or are going. The old linear progression of learn–work–retire has disappeared. The concept of lifelong learning is now replacing the old expectation that all education would be completed in your earlier years. If you initially trained as a carpenter in your teens, you might now, in your fifties, decide to have a crack at another career—perhaps as a lawyer—and if you successfully complete your degree (part time, in the evening, as a distance learner, whatever suits) and articles you can then practise. Instead of a straight career path, the course of our working lives is beginning to take on the irregular but far more stimulating shape of crazy paving.

Margaret Goodwin:
Drawing a life

I moved from Sydney to my current role as Marketing Manager for the Government of Yukon (Canada) in 2007. I love it. I'm not stuck in the office, but out and about in the Yukon.

I grew up in Glen Innes, New South Wales. We moved to the city when I was twelve and I attended North Sydney Girls High. I initially wanted to be a film director so I attended North Sydney TAFE where I gained a diploma in film and TV production. My first job was in the sound department of the ABC for four years where I assisted with film and sound editing. Next I went travelling to the UK on a working holiday for eighteen months. I sort of fell into the travel industry, starting as a reservations consultant with a Bali travel wholesaler. This gave me a foot in the door. My next job was at Trafalgar Tours where I eventually became a supervisor. In 1996 I went to Toronto where I filled in for the reservations manager. This was my first connection with Canada. I had to return to Australia when the contract was up but ever since I was on a mission to move back. In 1999 through word of mouth I learnt that the Canadian Tourism Corporation (CTC) was looking for somebody. I was overqualified for the original position but there was a new director of CTC in town who was looking for someone to work in the marketing area. Call it synchronicity, if you like. I took the job and worked as Marketing Services Manager for six and a half years, and got to visit Canada twice a year. Ultimately the job at the CTC became a means to getting what I really wanted, which was to move back to Canada. My boss, Donna, knew this was my ambition and said, 'Give me two good years of work and then I will help you get what you want.'

Why Canada?

I love the landscape, the mountains, the big, beautiful lakes and wild rivers. I am far more comfortable in this landscape than I am in Australia.

In a way I foretold this twice over.

First, when I did an exit interview at school and the principal asked me what I wanted to do. I'd seen a film on forestry in Canada, so I replied (God knows why), 'I want to plant trees in Canada.'

Much later, about six years ago, I went to a retreat on Scotland Island in Sydney, and we were asked to draw a picture of our ideal life. I drew pine and spruce trees in a wilderness with a big river, a small community and a camera, representing the photography I enjoy.

Later, I was standing on the deck, feeling at peace and thought, yes, I *am* going to go and live in Canada.

I recently found that picture and realised everything on that page is now a reality.

I don't really wish I'd made the move when I was younger. Everything happens at a time that is right. I also believe there is never a wrong career move. If you are clear about what you want, you will be subconsciously directing your efforts towards this goal, despite some detours. The real trick is to be clear about the goal. Describe it, or draw it in detail. What time you wake up, where you wake up, your breakfast and so on until you go to bed that night. This exercise really forces you to focus.

Margaret Goodwin is Overseas Marketing Officer (Asia/Pacific), Yukon Tourism and Culture

There are no barriers

In fact, there is nothing to stop you from applying for entry to any career course in the world.

Repeat, nothing.

So when you say to your friends and loved ones, 'I really wish I'd been a florist', you now have to be prepared to take ownership; this is something you can still do if it remains a burning ambition. And if you don't pursue this line of work, it is because you are choosing not to. Not because you are not 'allowed' to or you are 'barred' from this profession or because you cannot gain the qualifications 'at your age'. None of these reasons are even remotely defensible. So even if you resist the simplicity of the statement that all career aims are achievable, try to suspend your disbelief while you are reading this book and learning how to kick-start your next career.

In fact, those of us old enough to have experienced the linear education–work career path may need to readjust to the idea of seeing our own career progression as 'crazy paving' with simultaneous learning and working activities punctuated by time out, parenting, caring for others, volunteer work and travel. The old steady uphill path—until you reach the pinnacle—finally you've 'made it'—before a gracious decline into the dimly lit twilight years, no longer has to be your fate. There just has to be more to life than that. And there is—a myriad of challenges, adventures and fun to be had for those who wish to work longer, in different arenas. Recognising the random pattern of our working lives is the first step to freedom. This new 'randomisation' of work manifests itself in six very different ways:

- a shift of emphasis from money to meaning
- a shattering of the previous 'contract' of full-time job for life
- a dramatic change in the place and space where work occurs
- a change in the power relationship between company and worker
- a redefinition of job security
- a lessening of the relevance of age or stage of worker

Let's consider each of them.

From money to meaning

Many workers in western nations receive sufficient income to satisfy highly sophisticated needs as well as the basics of shelter, clothing and food. Their search for self-fulfilment is now often heavily attached to the quest for more meaningful work. Described by American transitional management specialist and author, William Bridges, this 'money to meaning' phenomenon particularly applies to those who have been in the workforce a long time. It can also be prevalent amongst recent university graduates. The reasons why workers at different ages or life stages might want a more meaningful occupation can vary. Older workers may have reached a level of maturity and/ or financial security where they feel they can 'afford' to give back; to leave a legacy of something more than an empty in-tray. Younger people, including graduates, may believe corporates are only interested in the bottom line, often at the expense of humankind, and so decide that their first work priority is to do something more worthwhile and to hopefully incorporate some life balance along the way.

RIP the full-time job

Sometime in the past 30 years something incredible occurred and most of us have missed it. A quick glance at Australian Bureau of

Statistics (ABS) research, however, reveals just how comprehensive the death of full-time paid work is. Where have these full-time jobs gone? To casual, part-time or temporary positions or contractual or consultancy-based projects is the answer. In *Tribes: We need you to lead us*, author Seth Godin calls this the 'Project Hollywood' way of working. To make a movie, a project is created, specialist workers are contracted and assembled where and when needed, and when the project is completed the whole team disperses. This is the way of the future. Jobs are going out the back door and 'work' is being performed as, when and in whatever way necessary. For some workers this will introduce an unprecedented freedom to their existence, and they will use this new way of working to shift employment hours to suit their personal needs and family schedules. Other workers will miss the structure, continuity and predictably of the day job. Some may never recover and will not find a place in the new work order.

It's also no surprise that, as the shift from money to meaning gains momentum, the term 'free' pops up in new descriptors for changed ways of working, in particular the terms free agent or freelance.

Place and space dissolve
The increasing fragmentation of the traditional day job has also had a massive impact on where and when work is performed. In 1998 Ira Matathia and Marian Salzman wrote *Next: Trends for the future*, in which they predicted the future of work and how it would be carried out. They were basing many of their conclusions on the 'cyber reality' of their advertising agency work, which was then at the cutting edge of work practices. Their predictions, however, have held true for a wide range of occupations across most industry groups. They described offices as depots that 'cut the cords of physicality', depots that workers might occasionally visit to report in, but are no longer necessary for the production of the work itself: that of 'hotdesking' where companies offer fewer desks than workers, and concentrate more on meeting rooms where the 'real' team work can be done. 'Virtuality will permanently alter the workplaces and working styles of

the future', they predicted. It has. The office is becoming the laptop computer, BlackBerry or iPhone, with work performed in cafés, on planes, at home, and, less often, in an office. For a while the serviced office was a popular façade for those who were setting up a new business and did not possess the resources necessary to fund their own bricks-and-mortar workplace. Trained staff would answer the phone, while a communal reception area and meeting place gave the impression of a larger organisation. But no longer does this need to impress figure so largely in the workplace. Many successful businesses are now conducted by phone or laptop, rendering the need for an office, or even the façade of an office, obsolete.

Time has also been fractured, partly by increasing globalisation where work teams need to provide around-the-clock support but also by the understanding that if the work data exists in cyberspace it can be accessed on demand—when the worker is best able to handle it—which is not necessarily between 9 am and 5 pm. Many mothers of young children perform their paid work when children are at school or asleep—not always during traditional company hours. The increasing erosion of a central workplace is not confined to high-tech industries but spreading to all occupations where a PDA (personal digital assistant) offers instant connection to central information. One example of this is parking officers who now do all their work in the street, with data relayed back to local councils or shires by wireless connections. These workers rarely find it necessary to visit the council office.

Goodbye mother ship

In the old 'job for life' days there may have been a sense of an all-powerful employer and an (almost) powerless wage slave. Judging by the advice available to would-be applicants before a job interview about how to dress, speak and perform to please, it would seem that the employer still holds all the power. This is very dated thinking. The world has changed. It was once the larger companies who employed the most workers. Now there are more small business owner-managers in Australia than any other category. Also on the increase are those who earn their dollars as consultants or contractors.

Whilst once a company might have adopted a paternalistic role and assumed responsibility for pension funds, health insurance and many other benefits, it has become increasingly common for shareholders to call the shots. And shareholders, according to market indices, seem to like nothing better than staff reductions and reduced obligations to those who remain.

Many companies have also found it much more profitable to outsource services and to hire consultants, freelancers, temporary workers or part-time or casual staff to do work on a project basis rather than making a long-term, and highly expensive, commitment to individual workers. This message has been received loud and clear by younger employees who treat jobs as short-term assignments rather than exercises in mutual loyalty. Workers of all ages and stages need to understand this new reality:

- Old-fashioned loyalty is gone.
- You are as good as your last project.
- Your bargaining power is equal to the person on the other side of the table.

Not only can these be incredibly liberating thoughts, they also free you up to think of your career(s) as separate small businesses which need to be personally and actively managed on an ongoing basis.

And if you are already an owner-manager, although at times you may feel beholden to your clients, the advantage is that you (hopefully) have more than one.

Redefining security

As we have seen with the demise of the job for life, the concept of work security, too, has largely disappeared. This may seem a frightening thought, but it is one most workers will need to get their heads around. If you are searching for job security you are seeking security in the wrong place. Remember, the job is dead. From now on you need to stop looking outside and start looking to yourself to create new conditions. These new conditions will prove to be the only way to strengthen your work security. They involve a process of understanding your best work attributes, supplementing those skills which are necessary in today's work environment, staying abreast of developments in your field, or fields, of choice, and keeping your professional or vocational networks current. In short, to remain work-secure you must remain work-relevant.

Work at any age or stage

Age and stage are becoming less relevant, with retirement as we knew it officially obsolete—but more about this in Chapter 10. The old linear progression of education–work–retire has been so shaken up that workers may now acquire their highest educational qualifications towards the end of a formal work career—and this qualification might lead to new directions or businesses. The concept of project-based work, rather than jobs, will demand the best person is hired, whether that person is a 22-year-old nerd—or a 75-year-old grandmother. It will come down to suitability for the (short-term) role. And if applications are handled by an online search engine, the demeanour of the grandmother probably won't count against her as it might have done if an ageist recruitment specialist was involved.

Once we understand and accept these six influences on the way we work and our career paths, we can enjoy the ride rather than feel threatened by the change.

Connecting the career dots

If we accept the 'crazy paving' concept of career progress, does this mean it is more challenging than ever to create an exciting career change? Does too much choice in the ways we can work just make the whole career planning scenario even more problematic? While from the outside it may appear overly confusing, understanding the mechanics of career change will better enable you to plan and achieve a smooth transition towards the career you desire. Effective career change begins with the recognition and analysis of the six main factors which are always present in the work you do:

1. the sector and/or industry in which you work
2. the organisation which employs you (government, not-for-profit, private or public company, association, own business)
3. the specific role and tasks you perform
4. your work arrangement (full time, part time, permanent, casual, contract, consultant, project-based, or portfolio)
5. the location(s) (external office, home office, virtual office, field work or mix)
6. the learning involved (education, qualifications, training, experience).

Some people who seek change really want the full enchilada—a leap from a specific role in a specific location to an entirely different type of work engagement somewhere else. This happened when former marketing manager, Tara Burns, resigned from her role in a capital city with a large IT company to become self-employed, starting a bed & breakfast in a small coastal town. This is a dramatic 'six-factor' change which, when considered in terms of Table 1.1, Connecting your career dots, shows a change in each and every element of the work Tara did:

1. sector—from IT to hospitality
2. organisation—from public company to startup home-based business
3. specific role—from marketing manager to B&B owner/manager
4. work arrangement—from full-time paid employee to full-time (plus non-paid overtime) self-employment
5. location—from large city to small town
6. learning—from frequent use of formal educational skills (marketing degree) to infrequent use of same skills, now supplemented by new hospitality skills and interpersonal communications skills.

Your appetite for risk

Not everyone is like Tara with the appetite for such a seemingly high-risk six-factor change. Many would prefer a gentler career segue which involves a change in just one or two elements—such as a new role with the same employer, perhaps a move to another branch of the same company, or the undertaking of some training or short courses to extend their experience in a new sector.

Regardless of whether your desired work change is dramatic or subtle, Table 1.1 will assist you to think more objectively about the moves you might make. By defining possibilities in each of the six categories, you can then evaluate the magnitude of the changes you might make and consider the pros and cons of such dislocation *before* leaping in feet first. The table also enables you to prioritise possible changes in the most 'do-able' order, so you are managing your future career changes in an ongoing series of smaller steps.

This method has two important benefits. First, it allows you to navigate change in a way that is manageable rather than threatening and in a way which complements other aspects of your life. If you can demonstrate that it is a carefully considered step in a grander plan, it's less likely to frighten the family!

Second, it means that you have stepped onto a professional development escalator, acknowledging the need to continue to learn and develop.

If you are prepared to stay *on* the escalator, you will remain employment-relevant for the rest of your life.

Your current situation

Make a start now by listing your current situation under the six different 'career dot' categories, remembering to include in the *Learning* category whether you are currently undergoing a training or professional development program.

Next, list four or five potential changes you might make in *each* category. As you read the following chapters, and see how others have successfully connected *their* career dots to find more meaningful

Table 1.1 Connecting your career dots

Sector	Organisation	Next steps
• (current)	• (current)	1.
•	•	2.
•	•	3.
•	•	4.
•	•	5.
•	•	6.

Specific role	Work arrangement	
• (current)	• (current)	
•	•	
•	•	
•	•	
•	•	

Location	Learning	
• (current)	• (current)	
•	•	
•	•	
•	•	
•	•	
•	•	

work, you can revisit the table to amend these options as often as you like. The more you think outside the square and actively review each of the six factors, the more likely you are to come up with an interesting and achievable path to a new and more satisfying way of working. This table can be photocopied for multiple uses. It is also downloadable from the website <www.what-next.com.au> so it can be saved as an electronic document.

When you have considered some of these very different ways of making work *work* for you, then use the right-hand column, titled 'Next steps', to prioritise moves you will make during the coming year— be they a change of sector, organisation, role, work arrangement, location or learning. As the many people profiled in this book can and will testify, there is no one 'right' way to make a significant work change—and no preferred 'order'. But thinking through what feels comfortable and what suits you most at this stage will help you identify at least one action to get you on your way!

How did Trevor do it?

To help get you started, let's revisit Trevor's story and connect the career dots behind his move from underground mine mechanic to an astronomer with his head well and truly in the stars.

The critical intersection in the above 'crazy paving' is that of Trevor's mechanical skills and experience, which enabled him to build a telescope and his total passion to see whatever the night sky might reveal.

And Margaret?

Margaret Goodwin's career change was driven by her long-held dream of living and working in Canada. She had a taste of this in her younger years and this vision never receded. She worked within the travel sector, gained experience and seniority and then sought the employer most likely to help with her move—the Canadian Tourism Commission. Patient planning finally paid off with a job offer from the Yukon Government in 2007.

Table 1.2 Trevor's career dots

Sector	Organisation		Trevor's steps
• Mining	• BHP		1. Pursued hobby
•	• Nil		1. Informal learning associated with astronomy
•	• Self		2. Took package
•	•		3. Formal learning (distance degree)
•	•		4. Professional development—links to other astronomers
•	•		5. Home-based business
Specific role	**Work arrangement**		
• Mechanical	• Full-time employee		
• Electrical	• Redundancy		
• Refrigeration	• Self-employed		
• Hobby astronomer	•		
• Qualified astronomer	•		
Location	**Learning**		
• Broken Hill	• Apprenticeship 1		
• Broken Hill	• Apprenticeship 2		
• Broken Hill	• Apprenticeship 3		
• Distance Learning (telecommute)	• Hobby astronomy		
•	• Degree		
•	•		

Chapter wrap

It can feel scary out there, but only if you're out of touch, unprepared, or unwilling to prepare. The world of work has evolved more rapidly during the past three decades than in the 70 years prior. Whilst change can be unsettling, the changes in the way we work have given most people the opportunity to work in a much less formal way as well as affordable access to training, education and information. This means we have much more power over our own work future. By understanding and accepting the change which has occurred and learning the mechanics of the career change process you, too, can move toward more meaningful work—it's just a matter, like Trevor and Margaret, of successfully Connecting *your* career dots.

And one more thing.

Get set for more change. In fact, try to enjoy it.

It's not just inevitable, it's ubiquitous!

2

Shift happens

In 1970 when Alvin Toffler wrote the bestselling and prescient *Future Shock* he described technology as the 'great growling engine of change'. This was well before PCs had become common tools of trade and the internet had begun to offer the main method of workplace communication. Even Toffler's wildest dreams could not have foreseen the shift in the last 30 years in the speed and reach of communications via the internet. This shift, more than most, has had a dramatic impact on all aspects of our working lives. The obvious changes—where we work and how we work—mean increased flexibility in delivery. Less obvious is the way the lack of hierarchy within the online world has threatened the former 'command and control' management structure of employers, particularly larger organisations. Increased flexibility, driven by new technologies, is a positive, but only for those prepared to embrace technology. Those who refuse to adapt will find themselves quite literally out of the loop. If you wish to remain employable, the choice is yours.

Wearing IT

Everything old is new again. It's 1709 and Richard Steele and Joseph Addison are collaborating on a newsletter which discusses current trends in politics, manners, society and entertainment in the City of London under the reign of Queen Anne. Their journal is titled *Tatler* and Addison has a lot of free time to work on it, as he has recently lost his secretaryship when the Whigs lost political control. 'Out of office and keeping a low profile' he writes his columns from different parts of London, as does Steele who filed copy on 15 April from 'my own Apartment', 18 April from 'Will's Coffee-house' and jointly with Addison on 20 May from 'St James Coffee House'. It is easy for these two gentlemen to be nomadic workers—they wear the IT of the day (feather quills) lightly.

Fast forward 300 years to 2009. In the intervening centuries the tools of trade were collected into factories and offices where workers gathered daily to produce. Only in the last 20 years has technology become sufficiently affordable and portable for us to once again wander while we work.

To interview the first expert for this chapter, it seemed only fitting that I should replicate the modus operandi of Addison and Steele, and so in early June, Graeme Philipson and I met in a coffee shop in Sydney, wearing our technology slightly less lightly (BlackBerry, mobile phone, notebook computers, tape recorder) and sharing thoughts on trends in society and work. It's taken three centuries, but we have come full circle to the coffee house model of work.

Plus ça change, plus c'est la même chose . . . (The more things change, the more they stay the same . . .)

Graeme Philipson
Pay per performance

The long-term prognosis for the human race is not good.

We are living in the last generation of humans who will be the dominant life form on this planet. The value of humans won't diminish in the immediate future because we still need humans to sift and evaluate information, but it is only a matter of time before 'knowbots' take over. The rate of increase in artificial intelligence

(AI) and intelligence in digital devices will exceed intelligence in humans in 30 years.

Just think back to how it was before PCs, prior to the 1980s when no one had one. By the end of the 1980s virtually all white-collar workers used a computer. This was the standard for twenty years and has resulted in a vast improvement in office productivity, particularly associated with word-processing and spreadsheets. The typing pool has gone—people are their own secretaries.

The 1990s saw the arrival of the internet and mobile technology. At the beginning of the 1990s virtually no one was online. At the end of the 1990s we all were.

We now use the internet for all sorts of things. It's so common that the 'e-' prefix (e-commerce, e-communication) has disappeared. Next came the mobile phone which moved from unheard of in 1990 to all-pervasive in ten years.

From 2000 to 2010 we have moved from voice to SMS to digital data and a spread of wireless data, wireless hotspots and LANs (local area networks). Many workers are now based remotely from their offices and telecommuting is common.

From the 1980s until now we have seen a total and utter transformation in the way individuals work. Technology, which was previously confined to back offices, was expensive and the preserve of corporates.

There has been a comprehensive democratisation of knowledge and IT.

The old-world industrial business model was based on the transfer and sale of physical goods. Scarcity meant something was more valuable. This notion is gone. The information world has changed everything including the economic law of supply and demand. Information is now infinitely replicable at no cost. This has had an impact on the old-world laws of copyright where intellectual property (IP) was able to be owned, sold and protected.

Now we think it should be free and available, leading to 'copyleft' which includes the huge business of open-source information and software.

We are reverting to a 'pay per performance' model which existed long ago. Artistic creators such as Shakespeare, da Vinci and Bach created a piece for a time which was then performed or reproduced. Copyright in eighteenth-century England came into being to preserve the rights of the publishers, not the authors. The internet is eroding the copyright model for words and music, as evidenced by the number of artists who now need to go back on the road to earn income.

People who are fighting against this 'pay per performance' model are fighting against history and technology. As the Luddites discovered when they broke stocking frames in the early 1800s, it simply doesn't work.

There are advantages and disadvantages with these technologies. They have certainly made work more interesting and more diverse. The complexities are a fabulous challenge and we all have the world's largest library at our fingertips.

The downside is the proliferation of dross—the new social networking site, Twitter, has definitely upped the crap factor. There is also a lot of erroneous information and harmful material and an increase in spam and cyber crime.

Technology is changing so quickly and forcing change on so many aspects of our lives. Everyone's modus operandi needs to be based on the fact that change is a constant. Nothing is stable; not your job, nor information, nor the way you receive that information or the cost of the technology that delivers it.

Graeme Philipson is Research Director of Connection Research <www.connectionresearch.com.au>

Technology rules

On a daily basis. The analogy of a frog in boiling water serves to remind us that we don't see change until the moment that it can destroy us. For many non-technically-minded workers, the change in the way we receive and manage information is confusing at best, and downright terrifying at worst. Change can feel uncomfortable at any time and change based on incomprehensible algorithms and intangible 'wireless' transmission seems too difficult to bother to understand. But an understanding of the way technology is shaping our future work prospects is vital to those who wish to remain in work and in demand in the near future. It is no longer a matter of whether we choose to adopt new technology; new technology has adopted us.

The digital public square

When Barack Obama was elected forty-fourth president of the United States there was a lot of media coverage about his colour—as the first black man in the Oval Office—and nearly as much about his BlackBerry—as the first president to be comfortable with tools of the digital age. But such discussion has masked an even more important change in the White House administration: a determination to understand and, further, to employ the functions of Web 2.0 to create a 'digital public square' offering an unprecedented access to government data and a new attempt at transparency.

We can see this with the appointment, by the Obama administration, of a Chief Information Officer (CIO), Vivek Kundra and a Chief Technology Officer (CTO), Aneesh Chopra for their understanding of the digital public square. Both men had previously served at state government levels, using new technologies to deliver a two-way government–citizen conversation online. Now they have been given the chance to do this at a national level.

Twitter revolution

On 4 June 1989, the Chinese Government ordered the execution of an unknown number of students and civilians who were protesting in Tiananmen Square in Beijing. The rest of the world learnt of this by radio and a few grainy photographic or televised images which were smuggled out.

Twenty years later, almost to the day, on 17 June 2009, a groundswell of protest against the results of the Iranian election was seen online around the world, despite vigorous attempts by the Iranian Government to deport journalists and electronically jam the internet. Not only were the protests reported online, the use of Twitter and Facebook meant they were orchestrated online as well with protesters posting their whereabouts, alerting other citizens about planned demonstrations and uploading video images taken with mobile phones. BBC Persian television reporter, Sadeq Saba, described this situation as 'witnessing the first electronic revolution'.

'And this movement is probably . . . the first kind of electronic revolution or electronic peaceful movement in the world, because new technology is playing a big role in the demonstrations, before and during the election.'

No longer clueless

The Cluetrain Manifesto: The end of business as usual was written in collaboration by four US-based IT veterans (Rick Levine, Christopher Locke, Doc Searls and David Weinberger) in 1999. First published on a website of the same name, the 'sequel' has since been published in print; a series of 95 theses, termed a manifesto as an homage to the letter Martin Luther pinned to the door of the All Saints Church in Wittenberg, Germany, in 1517. The authors seemed to suggest that their way of viewing the online world would have a similar impact to that of Luther's new world order, the Reformation. And in a secular way, they were right. Ten years later their succinct and witty take on the way the internet has become a 'global communication system that restores the banter' of ancient bazaars is still recognised as an eloquent and authoritative understanding of the power of social networking online. Their introduction declares that 'people are discovering and inventing new ways to share relevant knowledge with blinding speed' and all four authors proceed to demonstrate how the old hierarchy of powerful companies and powerless consumers has been subverted, if not inverted, by the nature of hyperlinks. The only image in *The Clutetrain Manifesto*—one of a dead skunk in the middle of the road—illustrates perfectly their contention that old style 'command and control' management is dead—killed by the internet.

David Clarke:
Setting the limits

I'm 62 and have been running Webjet for ten years now. After I left school I completed an accountancy certificate by correspondence, then worked at Myer, before moving to the transport industry. I was with Jetset Travel Group from 1977 to 1995, initially in accounting before moving to the role of Group Chief Executive.

Then I retired. Cold turkey. I was never bored, although my friends had warned I would be. I was very happy for three years just relaxing, travelling and reading. This could have continued indefinitely, but I had an idea.

During my time in the travel industry I had noticed there were so many layers involved in a sale, including the supplier, the wholesale, the ticketing and so on. Communication was inefficient (faxes!), expensive and not easily globalised.

Around 1995, as the internet started to develop, it became clear it would be possible to harness this form of communication as a virtually free channel. Far better delivery of travel product would be economically possible. We could put the booking into the hands of the customer and cut out the layers.

By 1998 this concept had become even clearer so we created a business plan and gathered a syndicate of investors. Webjet was launched commercially at the beginning of 1998. Two years later we listed on the stock exchange.

It was never a question of making a business *out of* the internet, it was a business conducted *on* the internet. This was one principle I felt strongly about and stuck with. We planned to stick around—not to be captured by venture capitalists. It was never a 'build and flip' exercise.

Ask yourself, 'How much am I prepared to risk both financially and in terms of time?'

If you can't decide these two things, don't do it.

Webjet offers a strong set of value propositions which recognise that consumers are more sophisticated and capable than many businesses think. Consumers wish to do business in *their* time at *their* convenience, not the convenience of the corporation. They also want to free themselves from the selling pressure and biases of retailers—a shift from subservience to control. This makes the wholesale travel agent proposition unsustainable as well as costly.

The technology behind our brand was a challenge. We approached it with a series of small steps using all available utilities, basically offshoots of existing airline software systems. But these systems were dinosaurs. We needed to develop our own booking engine which would handle travel service aggregation of diverse airlines, hotels and car rentals. We had limited capital—about $1 million in the bank—so we approached Microsoft. Our approach coincided with the establishment of a new industry solutions department—the Solutions Development Centre. So we commenced a $2 million fixed-price project, and funded it with extra capital from Galileo (an airline booking system company) which would receive use of the new software in a non-competitive zone.

This was a really exciting time. Galileo thought it would cost $10 million and take five years for this same project. Our joint

Microsoft project was delivered within a year—on budget and on time. The project assumed a life of its own. All partners invested a huge level of commitment. It was massively challenging but one of those magical commercial moments.

My role today is that of managing director, which means strategy, investors and ASX matters, principal stakeholders and guiding management through our CEO. Although at heart I'm a marketer. I believe brand value is paramount.

Do I have advice for others interested in a similar business startup?

It's important to ask yourself, 'How much am I prepared to risk both financially and in terms of time?' Once you make these decisions you can move forward with other considerations. If you can't decide these two things, don't do it. It's like gambling. Don't double your bet. Set the limit and work within it.

David Clarke is Managing Director of Webjet
<www.webjet.com.au>

Future directions?

So what will technological advances mean for the workplace of the future? Based in California, USA, the Institute for the Future is an independent non-profit research centre, which studies future trends and discontinuities. In 2007 the institute published a report titled *The Future of Work*, which included a 58-page document titled *Perspectives* aimed at identifying and evaluating technological innovations and their impact on work for the next three to ten years. The report identified seven underlying work-related technologies:

- proactive computing
- amplified collaboration tools
- sensemaking and visualisation

- device webs and sensor webs
- ubiquitous displays
- abundant computing and connectivity
- 3D graphical interfaces

And it predicted six work themes which would emerge from these directions:

- collective intelligence
- crowd sourcing
- common languages across disciplines
- need for collaboration/teamwork
- project-based work
- 'self agency'

Whilst the technical detail of these changes/innovations can be complex, the message is short, sharp and succinct. New technologies are forcing irrevocable change on the way we measure and value work. In particular, the former (developed world) notion of a fair day's pay for a fair day's work is finished. A shift is occurring which transcends the changes in machines, software, functions and channels of transmission. This shift is from the old-style hierarchy of bosses and workers to a new-style cooperative which values inputs from whomever can best deliver at a particular time. The message from the institute is clear. If you are prepared to work on becoming a knowledgeable or skilled 'deliverer' your working future looks rosy.

Tapping the wisdom of the crowds

Whilst crowd sourcing and collaborative projects may seem remote concepts, many of us in fact are regularly involved in such activities already. Websites such as Wikipedia and computer software bulletin boards or food websites that invite recipes are all tapping into the wisdom of 'citizen authors' to gather and share content. Many workers are already collaborating and contributing via a company intranet. Other workplaces encourage their people to join in the conversation using an instant messaging program on sites such as Facebook or Yahoo! or MSN. Sydney-based Yahoo!7 employee, Anthony, is constantly updated by work colleagues with news both trivial and important—including whether to avoid travelling across the Harbour Bridge because of heavy traffic. He considers the use of messaging a vital tool of his trade.

Another trend which has arisen from the growth in telecommuting and a newly empowered nomadic workforce is the advent of 'hotdesking', where companies provide fewer desks or workstations than the volume of workers on their books. This term derived from hotbunking (or hotracking), a word describing the practice of different people napping in the same bunks on navy ships over the course of different shifts. With more and more workers telecommuting, companies have seen the massive savings to be made in real estate and office services by providing communal desks and meeting rooms instead of spaces dedicated to a single worker. As technology has reduced in size, many workers now carry their desk (top) as a PDA or notebook computer.

Taking the 'man' out of manual

Advances in technology aren't restricted to the territory of knowledge workers. Those in the service and manual sectors are experiencing changes as well. As we will see in Chapter 10, one truck manufacturer in North America took note of the ageing workforce and, rather than ask 50-year-old assembly line workers to crawl under trucks, they decided to invest in machinery to 'flip the trucks' upside down. Similarly, in some hospitals a robot now performs the task of lifting and transferring patients confined to beds, saving the backs of older hospital workers.

New technologies such as these tell us three things. First, even the heaviest of tasks are no longer breaking the backs or bodies of manual labourers. The design and implementation of labour-saving devices means the work can be managed by men or women who are physically strong, and equally well by those who are not. Second, protecting the physical wellbeing of older staff is very important to companies desperate to hire and retain skilled workers. And third, although there may be fewer jobs in sectors where machines literally 'pick up the load', there will be many more jobs in sectors such as the services industries, in particular aged care, where certain forms of human contact are imperative.

Your shopfront goes digital

Regardless of whether you work as a high-tech road warrior, connected to companies by wireless, or as an artisan in a bricks-and-mortar studio, there are two aspects of the internet which have the potential to have a strong impact on your work. The first involves using the internet in order to obtain work. And the second is all about how *not* to use it.

It may be that you are seeking work as a full-time paid employee or as a contractor or freelancer. Whatever the terms of your engagement, one of the ways you will apply or 'be found' will almost certainly involve a digital dialogue—the sending/uploading of a CV or a pitch for new business. One recent estimate for the time taken to peruse the average online CV is fifteen seconds. Given the lifetime of experience in your CV, the idea of 'random' selection via a search crawler happening to light upon a relevant word in your CV is pretty insulting.

The solution to avoid being a victim of such arbitrary selection is twofold. First, your online résumé or CV must be a succinct summary of you as a resource, a well-networked (connected) individual who has the ability to add value to a team. It must be an active outline or pitch of *how* your experience has and will enable colleagues to produce better work (see Chapter 7). And if we endorse the *Cluetrain Manifesto* belief that the hierarchical has been replaced by the hyperlink, what's to stop you filling your brief CV or application with hyperlinks to longer, more illustrative information about Brand You, such as your blogs, your work achievements and your networks?

The second strategy to ensure you cannot be overlooked when lined up beside thousands of other similar applicants is to refuse to make your online application your main pitch for the business in the first place. Don't put yourself in such an anonymous pool of talent. Design the role you want and approach the company before they advertise or send out feelers. It's called being proactive. Career consultants tend to be consistent on one point at least. Up to 80 per cent of jobs are never advertised. And this percentage refers only to paid employees rather than contracts. So if you are seeking a position as a contractor or freelancer or similar work project, the number of such projects *not* advertised is far, far higher. The internet is a great place to find out what is going on—but if you want the perfect role to come dressed up as an advertisement, you may be looking in the wrong places.

Pants down

This is how you don't want to be found. On your Facebook page, smashed on wine or peach vodka, mascara streaming, boobs falling out (female) or pants down, urinating (male). And yet this is how some of the 160 million workers on Facebook show their face, or worse, to the world. Do they really think prospective employers or colleagues won't Google them as a first-base check on their credentials? You *may* get away with this at the office party (unlikely) but using such images on your electronic calling card is just dumb. Conclusion? Everything you do or say or post or respond to online has the potential to be found and read by prospective employers, hirers, colleagues, employees. Try to resist shooting yourself in the foot electronically.

Fiona Cole
A different typewriter

A lot of younger workers blur the distinction between work and home and see no need to separate the two. They think the nine-to-five shift is a struggle and want a lot more flexibility in the workplace. If you're not having fun, why are you there?

Because the Yahoo!7 brand is young and fun and energetic there are few people aged over 40 in this company. You can be 50 or 60 and have energy but we just don't seem to attract older workers. This translates to a gross lack of management experience, leadership capability and maturity. Younger managers simply don't know how to handle older people. Their expectations are, if I'm managing someone older they will know more and be more confident and experienced.

Prospective employees need to be careful. Companies can and do search online and see where you have been, what your blogs say and so on. We also check sites such as LinkedIn—it's of interest to us who you are connected to. Teamwork and collaboration are still important skills—but I don't think that side of doing business has changed. What is different is the lack of planning. There is a real lack of proactive thinking in digital media, with reactive thinking replacing the planning.

In the more traditional IT world, planning was much more rigorous but the internet is not about steps and stages—the digital media market is extremely volatile. A five-year strategy? You're kidding. Even three years is dreamland. We try to work 'long term' but six months to a year is about the limit.

How do people get jobs?

They know someone who knows someone. The referral system is extremely important. Word of mouth accounts for up to 40 per cent of our hires. The other 60 per cent are a mix of placing ads on our own site, using a specialist digital media recruitment service, and sending newsletters to an internal database of about 8000 people who may have worked for us, or applied for a job previously and missed out. This is a good source of candidates. We are also aware of profiles on sites such as LinkedIn and Facebook.

Using technology doesn't necessarily mean you have to be tech-savvy. Technology has been dumbed down so anyone can use it. It's not that hard to remain workplace-relevant. In any office job you have to have computer skills—you're just using a different form of typewriter. In the twenty years I've been working I would say the skills and issues remain similar—whether customer service or back office systems or digital processes—our skills are just applied to a different form of knowledge.

Fiona Cole is Human Resources Director at Yahoo!7
<www.yahoo7.com.au>

New core competencies

As noted by the Institute for the Future and *The Cluetrain Manifesto* one of the most important shifts for individuals to recognise about work and technology is the democratisation which is occurring in the workplace. Decision-making and influence is shifting from a top-down (think Henry Ford) to a bottom-up (online forums and communities) model. Examples of the bottom-up push occur regularly as sites try to change their functions or business models and a reaction from the 'crowd' subverts this desire, as witness the revolt by Facebook users when the website management tried to use them to push advertising to their friends.

This shift will call for a raft of new core competencies, largely based on analytical skills. With IT resources becoming more common and accessible, the Institute for the Future suggests that the ability to absorb information, make logical connections and facilitate links between ideas, websites, articles and people is critical. Those with mathematical and statistical skills will be in hot demand to sort and arrange data. Those with analytic capabilities will be required to make sense of the data for general or in-house consumption.

A digital divide?

Increasingly cheaper access to the online world and massive increases in the amount of data able to be shifted to individual PCs or hand-held devices means the lowering of economic barriers to technology. Of the 1.3 billion citizens of China, at least half have mobile phones and a majority use these for access to the internet rather than computers.

The real barriers in the digital world may be of an attitudinal nature. Those who think they do not 'understand' the online world and deliberately resist this way of connecting will almost surely reduce their prospects of ongoing employment. As the cost of technology reduces so the number of software applications available in a diverse array of industries rises. Waiters now order food on touch screens, parking inspectors issue tickets from PDAs, farmers sow fields in tractors loaded with GPS devices, cartoonists draw straight to screen. Resisting the need to understand the basics of using a computer is akin to trying to stare down a tidal wave. Don't try to do it. You'll just get swamped.

Alison Armstrong:
I can do this

I knew I would love the online businesses before I started them. I love everything to do with the internet and I had a strong urge to do something entrepreneurial.

It all came together at the right time. I had the opportunity to take a redundancy from my job in investment banking in 2002 and I had a new baby. So it was time for a change. I spoke to a couple of business school contacts who had started their own businesses but

I based most of my planning on knowledge gained from a previous role with Rothschild Asset Management where I was a strategic adviser to the CEO, then head of e-business. I became more and more interested in the internet and aware of the opportunities for online gift businesses such as Roses Only. I thought, I can do this, but just needed the right product.

I was on maternity leave, sitting on the floor, bouncing my baby when the idea of chocolates entered my mind. No one in Australia was doing it—there were a lot of chocolatiers making chocolate, but I wanted to market chocolate. So I was off and running. Every summer the chocolate companies would stop shipping so I researched packaging and logistics and knew year-round delivery was do-able. A girlfriend and I put the business together but she pulled out at the last minute. She was working full time and couldn't quite pull the plug on her career. This worked out for the best as now I own 100 per cent of the business.

Originally I had completed an honours degree at Melbourne University, then an MBA at INSEAD in France. My MBA supplied all the 'missing parts' in business strategy and this all came together with my job at Rothschild. I knew a lot about software development and specifications and inventory management and reporting. My knowledge of accounting was theoretical, so my dad, who is a retired engineer, chipped in and managed the MYOB for me. When it came to Search Engine Optimisation (SEO) in order to improve the website ranking, I learnt on the job. Every time I tried to seek professional help I would find the advisers didn't seem to know much more than I had already garnered from other websites and forums. The best business decision I made was to get good advice on public relations. I paid a writer to create five or six press releases which have basically been used multiple times over three years and achieved maximum mileage for our brand.

When my husband accepted a work transfer from Melbourne to Dubai I was able to move, but still run Definitely Chocolate and another online business I had set up in the preceding three years—<esunnies.com.au>. I had a crisis of confidence after I had been in Dubai three years. I was scared I could never get back into the corporate world. I wanted to reconnect and upskill as well as find out more about the country in which I was living—I hadn't even spoken to a native Emirati. It took four sessions of life counselling on Skype with a Sydney counsellor, Catherine Lockhart, for me to be convinced that my online business skills demonstrated entrepreneurial ability. With Catherine's assistance, I rewrote my CV, applied for, and won, the role as Principal Consultant with The Government of Dubai. A typical day involves strategy development for the government authority, then dinner at home with my family followed by an hour working on the online businesses.

But doing two jobs and managing a family is too much. I'm starting to resent the online businesses even though they are what I love. I went back to work a year ago because I felt a strong urge to connect with my community in Dubai and give something to the country that I love. However, the workload is now pretty heavy and I think something will have to go.

Alison Armstrong is Principal of Definitely Chocolate and esunnies.com.au
<www.definitelychocolate.com.au>
<www.esunnies.com.au>

Nomads wanted

The Institute for the Future paints a dramatic picture of the move from the 'tethered' workplace to a world where we will wear our devices, allowing for a seamless interaction as we pass through different environments and activate local sensors. The technology we use today—laptops or notebooks—is already being downsized to smart phones and will become even smaller and smarter. The new devices will enable workers to project onto screens in different workplaces or public spaces, and to absorb or share information pretty well anywhere in the world. This will create a new type of 'nomadic' worker practice which allows for 'seamless personal productivity'. The institute boldly predicts a much reduced need for business travel which will rather neatly match the new call for sustainability. This prediction may be correct, although it is highly likely the desire of individuals to enjoy the stimulation of different cultures, climates and cities will outweigh this projected demise of road warriordom. Technology may well rule, but for many the enjoyable stimulation of face-to-face encounters with like-minded friends and colleagues in foreign climes remains a strong motivation for travel.

Your network index

Marina Gorbis heads up the Institute for the Future. In a recent online article she predicted the next decade will be one of extreme organisational change and experimentation for society and commerce. In particular she notes the rise of the 'Amplified Individual', someone who derives their power from connections to the collective resources and intelligence of multitudes of others. The ability of these individuals to connect and rally is what gives them power along with the ability to bypass traditional organisational structures and boundaries. This leads to a new way of evaluating workers' or suppliers' strengths, using a Network Intelligence Index (NII). It's not so different from the old concept of someone having a strong (and vocationally useful) network—it's just likely that a lot of the connections will now be supported and strengthened by online communication. Most of us have a realistic sense of our own NII, but find it much more difficult to know how to enhance our networks. There is no simple answer to this need, as the 'amplified' individual's networks will vary widely according to their industry and position within it. The key learning is that all of our networks—personal, professional, electronic—need to be fostered and continually renewed in order for us to stay both connected and valuable to employers and hirers in general.

How's *your* NII?

New freedoms = tougher management

The new freedoms which flow to workers from the inversion of the old 'command and control' management structure sound seductive. Work anywhere? At any time? Sounds like an ongoing party, collaborating with buddies online and getting paid for it? I'm there!

But, sadly, all things come at a cost. And as generations of parents have told teenage children when they introduce the notion of curfews and responsible attitudes to alcohol, new freedoms can only mean one thing. New responsibilities.

If technology is indeed forcing hirers (employers or contractors) to pay by output, then the onus to deliver has been moved squarely back onto the shoulders of the employee or freelancer. If you have agreed to produce a certain amount of work by a due date for a fee, guess what? It's entirely up to you to do so, or forfeit the fee. So the new world of work will demand another, rather more old-fashioned set of skills: those of self-management. This is where you will need to enhance or adopt the skills of goal setting, task management and scheduling in a highly organised and rigorous manner. The tools which make this organisation easier are on a computer near you, but the willpower is something you will have to muster up yourself. Yep, the new freedom is great, but it comes at a price.

Resisting the blur

Separating work and play is the greatest skill of all. Having 24/7 access to your office, your colleagues or international contacts means they have the same access to you. If you are unable to set limits and guard your free time, you will have none. Those who don't take a break from work soon learn how stale they become. The ideas no longer flow, the work becomes a chore and everything seems to take longer. To protect your creativity and energy, and, more importantly, your relationships, you'll need to learn how to resist the blur that too much technology can foster.

Chapter wrap

Presenting the Boyer Lectures in Sydney in January 2009, the man who has amassed a fortune from newspapers, Rupert Murdoch, offered his advice regarding new technologies, telling his audience, '. . . whingeing about the technology will get you nowhere. The only way to deal with new technology that upends your job or your business model is to get out in front of it. Otherwise it will get out in front of you.'

And that's about the size of it. The need to understand and use new technology is non-negotiable for anyone wishing to remain employment-relevant. This need is not confined to office or knowledge workers, but includes all who want to know what is happening in their own corner of the world of work. We all need to maintain our basic technological skills; age or previous experience is no excuse. The stories of David Clarke and Alison Armstrong and their web-based businesses are reminders of how our 'day' jobs can teach us skills and expose us to knowledge that can be enhanced to create a new business concept. Both offer examples of the combination of technology with perceived demand to create something new, viable and profitable. But these opportunities only arose because the individuals concerned embraced the possibility of technology and made it their business to learn more.

Connecting the career dots

Although at very different ages and career stages, David and Alison both chose internet business startups for their next career moves. David came out of retirement but stayed in the same sector of travel to create a business with a new form of distribution. His location didn't change, but his preferred work arrangement was self-employment. His learning experience was 'on the job', understanding how Webjet could use new technology to deliver an entirely new way of buying travel products. Alison saw an opportunity to sell product online, but clearly understood the difference between selling a product and marketing it. Her learning involved research on the logistics of year-round delivery which gave her company, Definitely Chocolate, its competitive edge. A major relocation from Melbourne to Dubai had no impact on her ability to continue to manage her online business, merely requiring an adjustment to different time zones and increased use of Skype.

3

What makes you tick?

The key to finding work that is more satisfying and meaningful is to know yourself well. This involves three main actions. First, be prepared to take responsibility for your future career directions. As stated in the introduction, whatever has been the nature of your working life to date *does not* have to become a predictor of your future possibilities. It is important and highly profitable to see past experience as just that—past.

Second, allow yourself to turn a new page and write a new future based on the things which matter most to you today. To do this, you will need to gain a clear understanding of what success means to you and the values which you hold to be most important. Third, armed with this heightened self-awareness, you will be well placed to consider your personality traits and those skills you enjoy using the most.

It is only when we define our key motivations that we are able to ensure they are woven into the fabric of our working lives.

Who's in charge here, anyway?

Finding satisfying work is not easy.

But it *is* rewarding.

You can use many strategies to further your search and the following chapters offer some which may suit you. But it's not a one-way street. You, too, have to put in some hard work. And there is one key understanding which is non-negotiable. Unless you are prepared to recognise, respect and observe this maxim, it's unlikely you will fully maximise your own personal potential.

Those who do understand it will discover or confirm a simpler approach to most of life's challenges, many of which lie beyond the arena of work.

The key concept to understand and implement is that of the *locus of control*.

Susie Farmer:
Other people's agendas

I'm not really where I want to be. I trained as a pastry chef because that was one of the few courses for which I qualified. My parents were very forceful about me taking the course; they insisted I needed a trade in life. I wasn't a great student, I've always been slightly dyslexic, and passing exams was difficult. Anyway, I qualified and fell in love with a guy who didn't love me back. He was in the mining industry and I followed him around until I finally got the message that he wasn't the marrying type. Funnily enough this changed when he met his next girlfriend—he married her within a year! Then I met Ben and we got married within six months. I guess I was grabbing at security and it was nice to have someone who adored me for a change. Ben qualified as a vet and while I had been happy to move from country to city when I went to technical college, Ben was a city boy just dying to live in the country. So we moved back to the town in which I was raised. It's not exactly exciting after Brisbane. I've never really used my culinary skills; instead I work as a receptionist in Ben's clinic. I guess I've never really used any skills that I think I'm

---

really good at. I wouldn't say our marriage has been a particularly happy one either, but I didn't think it was that bad until about a year ago when Ben decided to leave me. He travelled for a while, and then came back, but we live in different parts of the house, and I am just waiting for him to go again. Meanwhile we continue to work together. I wouldn't say either of us is very fulfilled, so I guess it's a good thing we weren't able to have children.

(*Susie's name has been changed*)

A realistic sense of control

Attributed to the work of Julian Rotter in 1954, a locus of control (LoC) refers to an individual's perception of the cause of significant life events—whether they were caused by internal factors (your decisions and/or actions) or external ones (Acts of God, fate or destiny, or more powerful people, whether individuals or groups). A combination of behavioural and cognitive psychology, it was described by psychologist Philip Zimbardo, in 1985 as '. . . whether outcomes of our actions are contingent on what we do (internal LoC) or on events outside our personal control (external LoC)'.

Unsurprisingly, our psychological health is said to be improved if we have or can adopt an internal LoC. However, there is a strong need to balance an internal LoC with competence, efficacy, and opportunity. In other words, it is not sufficient within itself to believe you can control your own destiny—you must equip yourself with the skills, efficiency and opportunities to make advantageous things happen.

It is also useful to understand that possessing a strong internal LoC is not a Pollyanna-ish 'I can make anything happen' approach to life, but rather a realistic comprehension that there are some things which are totally beyond our control, and others which are very much within it. Acts of God such as tornadoes, bushfires and tsunamis are not something we can prevent or schedule. They have been occurring since the beginning of time. They are, however, natural disasters, the effects of which we can plan to minimise when it comes to where and how we build our homes and the knowledge and preparedness of local governments.

Understanding *your* LoC is vital to understanding what you can do if you are not enjoying your current employment—whether this is due to too much or too little work, the wrong role or industry, poor remuneration, unreasonable management, unsupportive colleagues, or a lack of professional development opportunities. A useful exercise is to list all those aspects of your work which are least appealing, and then to define whether they are beyond your locus of control (external), or whether your actions might have some influence (internal). Next try to brainstorm ways of changing them from negatives at least to neutrals—if not positives.

Removing excuses

A clear understanding of your (realistic) LoC is also the fastest and most effective way of getting rid of poor excuses for putting up with a second-class existence and joining those acquaintances who seem to have enjoyed an extraordinary run of good luck—for decades or longer.

Now let's revisit the story of Susie and consider Table 3.1, which attempts to analyse her perception of the causes of her (lack of) luck in life.

Then think about your own situation.

Have you, like Susie, fallen into the 'Stuff happens, so what can you do?' trap?

Or are you prepared to refresh your thinking and take direct responsibility for the many aspects of your life that you *can* control?

Susie's tale is a true story as experienced by a 62-year-old woman who lives in rural Queensland. If it seems unremittingly bleak this is probably because she seems to believe herself to be a total victim of unfortunate circumstances which are going from bad to worse. She has also handed over the control in her life to others, whether

Table 3.1 Just luck? Or within your locus of control?

Life event/ situation (Susie)	LoC Internal (I) or External (E)? (Susie's perception)	Your life event/ situation	LoC Internal (I) or External (E)?	What could you have done? What can you do?
Poor secondary results	E—dyslexia			
Tertiary study	E—parents insisted			
Love life	E—he wasn't marrying type			
Country move	E—Ben's decision			
Work as receptionist	E—Ben needs me to fill this role			
Unhappy marriage	E—needed security after first breakup			
Marriage doomed	E—Ben will decide to go again			

her parents, her first love, or her husband. It is a very sad scenario, but not that uncommon.

Nor is her situation impossible to change. It will only change, however, when and if Susie decides to acknowledge her role in the decision-making process. And that delegating decisions to others is still in fact making a decision: to be passive and cop whatever 'fate'—or the external LoC—dishes up.

One heartening aspect of the LoC is that research indicates it is not an underlying personality construct available only to born optimists. Instead, it is largely learned, as a response to circumstances, or due to psychological and/or educational intervention. So, yes, whether we feel ready for the responsibility or not, it *is* possible to learn to take more control of our lives. And even better, our 'ownership' of control often strengthens as we age.

Now *that* sounds like old-fashioned wisdom.

Are you up for it?

What is your work-related LoC? Do things just happen to you? Are you continually overlooked when the exciting tasks and projects are shared? Try P.E. Spector's online work locus of control checklist (see Notes and Resoures for web address) for some useful measures of how you view your own influence on your working life.

All bets are off

What would you do if you could do anything?

The reason why this is one of the hardest questions in the world to answer is because it strips away all your excuses. However it's also a very exciting starting point.

Your initial response might include winning Lotto, retiring, sailing the world in a luxury yacht, drinking fine wines and never working another day.

Your chances of winning Lotto are minimal but even if you did, it's highly likely you would be bored within a few months of doing nothing meaningful with your life.

Another major difficulty responding to a question which removes all barriers is that the landscape is just too broad to contemplate. It's akin to being back at school and being asked to write an essay on any topic we like, or to paint a picture of any subject which appeals. We freeze before the easel—too many choices means it's too difficult to make a choice. So the answer is to narrow the discussion and introduce useful parameters to help explore your inner landscape in a focused and fruitful way.

Who are you?

Very few people take time to consider their own wants, needs and ambitions on anything approaching a regular basis. Instead we behave like good soldiers, kitting up each morning and marching off to do battle in the workplace—without doing ourselves the courtesy of checking whether we are still fighting a just and honourable war. In order to break the big question (who are you?) into manageable chunks, it's important to focus on your internal attributes: your idea of success, your values, interests, personality, attitudes, favourite skills and how you talk to yourself. These are the foundations of what makes you a unique human being. They are also the aspects of your personality which should be protected, not violated by working in a way that conflicts with them. Nothing is more important than living a life which is aligned with what matters most to you. Chapter 4 will consider your external attributes—your formal qualifications, your skills, your work experience and achievements. These external achievements are also very important aspects of Brand You—but as they are usually more attainable and negotiable than your core beliefs and sense of right and wrong, they are nowhere near as important as your inner values.

This chapter prompts you to consider whether your values, skills and desires are still being met by your current work, or if there is a gap—perhaps even a chasm—which indicates that some career fine-tuning is required. The end aim is to find the most useful crossover points within your values, skills and experience, and dreams. These crossover points are the critical recurring elements which can help illuminate your potential new directions.

What is success?

In western economies, the desire to be 'successful' is usually taken as a given; an all-embracing motherhood statement. But just as mother- (or father-) hood does not suit everyone, visible 'success' is not necessarily universally sought.

A first critical step in the process of understanding yourself is to know what motivates you. We are constantly bombarded with images of 'successful' people—often celebrities who are famous for being celebrities—and so it becomes difficult to work out our own personal sense of success as opposed to current societal values.

How do *you* define success? What works best for you? Whom do you consider to be successful? Yourself? Someone at the top of their profession? Or a close friend or family member who seems to have ideal balance and emotional support?

Recent research on factors which contribute to success has been summarised in an article in the *Harvard Business Review* by Laura Nash and Howard Stevenson. The four factors Nash and Stevenson defined as integral to success are:

- happiness
- achievement
- significance (positively affecting those you care about)
- legacy (helping others find future success)

The authors also suggest that viewing these factors as a kaleidoscope with all four varying in impact and importance at any one time is the most helpful way of seeking success. This requirement to multi-task on these critical factors may indeed be the key to a long-term sense of being successful. But those in 'career crisis' may also find it useful to define which one of the above aspects is the most important for them, and to work on that one as a matter of priority.

Which element of success are *you* are seeking most urgently?

Table 3.2 Defining success

Success factor	How do you define this?	Who do you know who has this factor?	How important is this to you on a scale of 1-10?	What can you do to increase this element in your life if you rate it more than 6/10?
Happiness				
Achievement				
Significance				
Legacy				

Jimmy Pham:
Building a family

I was born in Saigon (now called Ho Chi Minh City) in 1972 at the height of the Vietnam War. By the time I was two, my family had realised North Vietnam was likely to be victorious and this would have disastrous consequences for those in the south. My Korean-born father was able to secure papers for me and my mother to leave with him, and we went first to Singapore, then Saudi Arabia before settling in Sydney.

When I left school I tried many different jobs including selling vacuum cleaners, cleaning caravans, and working in video shops and a supermarket before completing a certificate course in tourism at Hayden College in Sydney.

We have always been working people with firm values about earning your keep and remaining independent.

When I graduated I was told not to apply to airlines or wholesalers but smaller companies where we would be more likely to get a job. But I didn't want to end up stuck behind a desk, so I applied to two airlines and one wholesaler, and landed a job with Concord International, which ran Travel Indochina.

I believe I was destined to be around Asia. Two years later, in 1996, the company sent me to Ho Chi Minh City. I stayed in a hotel in Central District One. One night I went for a walk and met four kids carrying coconuts in their baskets. Each had the same radiant smile—one I couldn't define. But it seemed to say to me that no matter what their destiny was, they wouldn't be defeated.

Aged about thirteen years, they slept on the riverbanks and paid to shower in an area that was located next to an open sewer. None of them had ever been to school. The Vietnamese term for street kids is 'dust of life'. It means that they will never belong; they will never settle. It was hard for me to understand, so I went to the market and bought toothbrushes, toothpaste and clothing for them. They thought a new sucker was in town, a big fat turkey. Who was I to question their interpretation? They had never met a foreigner who would love them unconditionally. If I was giving them things for free, why not think I'm a turkey or that there will be a catch?

I met with them regularly and lots of kids would drift in from everywhere.

I took them for a bowl of Pho, we drank Coca Cola, and I heard their stories.

For one instant I thought I could make a difference, that I could come back and help these kids. It was a totally spontaneous reaction; I had no detailed plan.

On my return to Australia I talked to my family and convinced them of my project. I realised I would need to become a tour leader based in Vietnam to do this. And so I applied to the competition, Intrepid Tours, and got a job, partly based on a question I was asked at the interview, 'Why do you want this job?' To which I replied, 'I want to make a difference.' And they said they would help and they have—they have been there for nine years!

For the next three or so years I was based in Saigon and helped street kids there, but this was not sustainable. I gave money ('fish') to about 60 kids, from Cambodia, Nha Trang and Sapa. It helped financially and we would sit and talk and share a meal and they probably picked up a few communication skills. But, as the proverb says, to help them on a long-term basis I really needed to teach them to 'fish' for themselves. The turning point came in Hanoi. Nine kids I was helping there were waiting for me when I finished a tour. They said, 'We trust you, but we need more. We need jobs. We want to do something more useful. We can't just hang around waiting for you between tours.'

We had so little money, no direction and no business plan. But we had each other.

KOTO (Know One Teach One) started with a promise to those nine kids. That night we talked long and late and it dawned on me that hospitality would offer the most transferable skills for these nine. The practical considerations proved incredibly difficult. I only had a few thousand dollars and had no idea how to set up a business and no idea about hospitality. We located premises for a sandwich shop in Hanoi. It was tiny; just 30 square metres. Here I taught the kids basic hygiene and got Mum to send me the *Woman's Day* cookbook for recipes. I also asked Uncle Toby's in Australia to donate bulk supplies of White Wings cake mix—which they did, boxes upon boxes.

And so I began an unexpected culinary journey. We had so little money, no direction and no business plan. But we had each other. The first class, Class One, was made up of the original nine street kids, plus an extra eight. Now we teach 100 children at any one time, and this will increase to 200 when we open in Saigon at the end of 2009. Fifteen classes, or 450 children, have passed through KOTO and I am proud to say I know them all. Each one will teach one more. This in turn helps their siblings and parents.

I'm not afraid of making mistakes—it's how you grow as a human being. But I have had to learn the importance of having infrastructure in place before moving ahead. I've recruited the wrong people. That was not their fault—it was my bad decision. And I over-promise. I want the kids to have everything and it often takes longer to come through. I am far too open with these ambitions.

The easiest thing was finding my cause. For a long time I felt part of a minority. This can happen when you settle in a new land and you are Asian—you are treated as part of a category—it's not so much about finding a cause but about finding yourself. But if you keep searching you find something you love more than yourself.

You just need to have faith. And to go back to basics to find a cause that's pure and simple.

Every day I go to work and I am greeted with smiles and kids who say 'Thank you for my future.' They are more important than me. But the main point is to keep it simple. People, westerners in particular, overanalyse. Australia may be a First World country but that's not always a good thing. There's a lot for us to learn from Asian cultures where they have so little but they have so much. They keep it simple.

Jimmy Pham is founder of KOTO
<www.koto.com.au>

Can you increase your 'success' factors?

Do you believe, as Samuel Goldwyn did, that the harder you work, the luckier you get? Recent research by author Malcolm Gladwell seems to confirm this belief. In his book, *Outliers: The Story of success* Gladwell has made a study of factors which contribute to the success of outstanding individuals. There is bad news—and good. Some of the factors over which we have no control do indeed matter: birth date, parental wealth, your IQ. But others do not matter a toss. He shares examples of many individuals who have battled adversity using the skills and gifts they naturally possess and ultimately made their mark. Gladwell firmly believes these success 'indicators', if studied more thoroughly, might be leveraged to dramatically increase an individual's chance of doing extremely well within a particular profession or calling. One indicator which he highlights and which, Gladwell asserts, is accessible to everybody, is the 10,000 hour rule—practise any career skill for 10,000 hours and you are bound to do it well—and stand out in your chosen career! Throughout his book Gladwell cites examples from the Beatles to Bill Gates of how we often attribute luck and genius to people who have, in fact, completed substantial apprenticeships.

Your values

Why are our values so important? Our values are the key to our existence—they are what we believe to be most important in life. Many of us confuse goals with values—they are related, but not the same. Our goals are ambitions—things we hope to achieve. Our values are the underpinning fundamentals—the beliefs about which we cannot negotiate, because they are based upon our very sense of right and wrong. They were not chosen—but assimilated from our upbringing and the hundreds or thousands of people who have passed through our lives and had an impact upon us. The list in Table 3.3 may help you to isolate those values which motivate you the most—and therefore sharpen your thinking about the type of work that will have the best fit with these core motivations.

Table 3.3 Your values		
Generosity	Humour	Social conscience
Kindness	Practicality	Spirituality
Helpfulness	Enthusiasm	Respect
Education of others	Team work	Autonomy
Money	Efficiency	People orientation
Security	Competitiveness	World view
Independence	Intellect	Local focus
Education for self	Creativity	Environment-consciousness
Variety/diversity	Intuition	Business mindedness
Curiosity	Excitement	Good corporate citizenship
Wisdom	Freedom	Learning
Reliability	Influence	Detail focus
Responsibility	Political activism	Power
Honesty	Friendships (many)	Influence
Loyalty	Pedantry	Physical wellbeing
Flexibility	Organisation	

Tick the values which matter to you, then circle the five most important of all ticked items.

Personal values guide your 'non-work' behaviour, but they also influence your work attitudes and preferences. This list is not complete—it is merely offered as a thought-starter for you to work out those values you consider non-negotiable, and those on which you might be prepared to compromise in order to enjoy a more satisfying work life. Consider which five are the most important— and those that might influence your work values and the sense of reward you derive from your current role. There are no right or wrong responses, just honest ones.

What floats *your* boat?

We all have interests. If we didn't we'd be dead, or chronically incapable of getting out of bed and functioning in something approaching a normal manner. What interests you? In fact, let's rephrase that, as 'interest' sounds far too passive a point on which to base a shift in career. What *excites* you? There are two broad schools of thought on making your passion your career. The first is a rather tight, negative persuasion that working in a field you love will mean your hobby is diminished by your continual exposure to it. The other view, more widely accepted by career counselling professionals, is that you are far more likely to enjoy your work if it correlates with things that truly excite you.

Linda White:
A way to go back

In 1967, when I was 20, I went to London. Those were the days when girls were meant to get married. I stayed there for five years and worked as a bookkeeper, returning to Australia for a few months in 1971, before going to Germany for four years. In 1975 I came back to Australia. A legacy of the Whitlam Government was free tertiary education, so I had the opportunity to pursue a degree full time, choosing Media Studies and Sociology at Macquarie University. But I couldn't get work—I was apparently too qualified.

I became pregnant and gave birth to my son, Jemi, in 1979. In 1982 we travelled to Italy. My friends had an empty house near a village called Trequanda in Tuscany. The deal was that I would renovate the house in exchange for living there with my young son, rent free. I spoke German, but not Italian. I had to learn on the job. I'm a risk taker, so I was fine with this. I developed a great relationship with the next door neighbours—two brothers, Loreno and Onedo Bindi, and their wives and families. Happily these neighbours decided they liked us and took us in as if we were their own.

My son went to the local school, called *l'asilo*. Most of the women did piecework. In the morning the children would have lessons, then a lunch, home-cooked by the mothers, followed by a snooze so the mums who worked could collect them as late as 5 pm. I grew vegetables, bottled preserves, and exchanged labour to survive. I also worked for a local beekeeper. I learnt my Italian under the grapevines—where lots of gossip was exchanged, so I was able to learn more easily. I couldn't take formal lessons; I was too busy supporting us. They called me *La Straniera*—the foreigner. I was the only foreigner in the entire area at that time. It was a very humbling experience. Trequanda was a very conservative, very insular community—my child was the key in.

And yes, I was lonely, sometimes frightened, and often humiliated about my (lack of) language skills. After four years the renovations were nearly complete and the owner wanted the house back. My son needed an operation and because the medical system in Italy was in crisis we returned to Melbourne. From then on I was always looking for a way to go back

In Melbourne I completed a Diploma in Education (one year full time) and taught new arrivals at the Brunswick Language Centre. Then I did a second degree, part time, in ESL, Numeracy, Literacy and Italian, studying part-time for five years. I married in 1989 and we moved to Wangaratta in 1990 where I became an Italian teacher at the high school for five years. The marriage, however, didn't last. It was in Wangaratta that I joined the Italian Teachers Network, a regional association which included many of the high schools in Victoria's north-east. It was a rich network and we enjoyed many school camps and concerts.

At Wangaratta High I met Sandra, another teacher and member of the network. In 1995 I moved to a role managing programs at the Albury-Wodonga Adult Community Education Centre (ACE). I managed the ESL, literacy and numeracy subjects. In 1997 I was asked by the manager of the general program if I would take a painting class to Tuscany. It was the centre's first such trip—and it got me back to Italy, and Trequanda. In 2000, my last year at the Adult Community Centre, Sandra and I established a niche Italian touring business, Si Italy. Our promise is to show travellers Italian history, culture and cuisine and take them to places that they would never normally reach. Through the centre I did courses in International Business, the MYOB accountancy package and First Aid. We both also completed bus driver training in Wangaratta.

It wasn't exactly smooth sailing, however. Our first brochure went out in September 2001, the week of 9/11 when the twin towers in New York were hit. This was followed by the collapse of Ansett Airlines and the SARS virus. But our biggest business glitch has been more recent—the global economic crisis at the end of 2008. We thought we were dead in the water by Christmas even though 2008 had been our best year ever. But things now seem to be looking up again and bookings are coming through.

We had always worked for other people and viewed business as a foreign land even though we had a lot of skills from teaching. But we had to convince ourselves it would work so we went away for the weekend to thrash it out. I see my partnership with Sandra as a real bonus. We are two very different people. Sandra is cautious and I am a risk taker. I had seen my son through university and had no dependants. I was prepared to borrow money against my mortgage and live on credit. It was scary but worth it. Now I'm out of debt. For the past three years we have both drawn a small, but liveable, salary. I really don't want anything else.

Linda White is Director of Si Italy
<www.siitaly.com.au>

What excites you?

Most of us can readily identify those things that fascinate us—but many of us have never considered that we might actually make money from working in these arenas. Take time now to write six things that excite you the most. Then write, without stopping to think too deeply, the complementary roles. If you're stuck, read the example of Debbie in the left-hand columns of Table 3.4. As they say, too much analysis can lead to paralysis, so take no more than five minutes to complete this task.

Your personality

Since 1923 when Freud emphasised the role of the psyche in human behaviour, the importance of personality has been given precedence over the expectation that people will usually conform. We all think we know our personalities, but do we? And how important is an understanding of the finer nuances of our personality before making a career choice? It can sometimes become difficult to separate personality from style, but it is useful to consider the differences.

Personality tests

Personality tests are often the first of a range of tests which a career counsellor or practitioner will request you undertake. There are a

Table 3.4 What excites you?

Debbie loves	Possible roles	You love	Possible roles
Films	Filmmaking Production Reviewing		
Travel	Travel writing Travel agent Travel-related websites		
Social justice	Not-for-profits Social journalism		
Reading	Librarian Bookseller English teacher		
Cookery	Food critic Chef Microbusiness Selling biscuits		

wide range of personality tests, and different counsellors will have different preferences. How much such tests can reveal about you, and how useful this information might be in a search for more satisfying work, is open to debate. Most career advisers think personality tests have their place in starting an individual's thinking about different types of work, particularly that which will prove satisfying. Some of the more common tests include the following:

- Myers-Briggs Type Indicator (MBTI)
- John Holland Self Directed Search
- Firo-B Workplace Indicator
- Strong Interest Inventory

These tests can be completed with the guidance of a career counsellor, or by accessing online, usually for a fee. See the Notes and Resources section for web addresses. However, it is important to note that there are myriad career personality, type and indicator tests on the internet. In fact, career searches seem to bring out the best and worst of websites. It is very difficult to gauge which will suit you, which are based upon credible research and which will offer the most helpful prompts for those seeking clarification about their possible career paths. Some of these tests are free and some request a small or large payment before you can proceed. There are no guarantees that you will be happy with the outcome, or that the tests for which you pay are any better than those offered free of charge.

Your favourite skills

In the next chapter we will look at your external attributes—your education, specific work skills, experience and achievements. However, it is important to note in the context of your 'inner being' that whilst you may have an impressive array of life skills, there will be a shortlist which you *really* enjoy exercising. Merely listing the things you *can* do is no indication of what you *want* to do. Out of your many and varied skills, which reveal the 'real you'? Which are the ones you really enjoy using? Are you a natural-born teacher or trainer—do you love interaction with people who are learning? Are you a natural actress—someone who can't wait for the thrill of getting up on a podium and presenting ideas and thoughts to a roomful of people? Perhaps you are a 'fixer'—someone who loves to take something old and broken and restore it to its former glory. You might be working as an accountant, but it is your 'fixing' skill, not your head for numbers, that pleases you the most.

List your five favourite life skills in the table below—and add a short note why you enjoy each particular talent.

Table 3.5 Your favourite life skills	
Life skill	**Why I enjoy using this skill**
1.	
2.	
3.	
4.	
5.	

Your sense of self

How do you talk to yourself? Are you kind? Or have you lost faith in your ability to achieve? This may seem like a strange question, but it becomes important when you are searching for new career directions. If your view of yourself is less than positive, it is likely to influence your aspirations and actions as well as the way others perceive and value you. Rating our own self-esteem is very difficult and hardly an objective science. It is, however, well worth the time it takes to consider your sense of self-worth if you are aiming to make reasonable decisions about what you are (or are not) capable of doing.

It is difficult, at the best of times, to make a bold career move. When your self-esteem is low, it is probably impossible. It may be more useful to work on the issues causing this lack of confidence before immersing yourself in a plan to change your working life.

Who can advise you?

How do you find out more about your career drivers? Some of us are very self-directed and happy to explore our internal landscape using books, internet tools and our own thoughts. Others may prefer to work with other people to pinpoint who they are and what makes them tick. Some good ways to explore your next career include:

- buying a recognised and credible career planning guide and completing the worksheets (see Notes and Resources section for some suggestions)
- using the internet
- face-to-face meetings with a trained career counsellor or psychologist, either within your organisation, or private practice

The granddaddy of job search

The 'granddaddy' of career search has to be Richard Bolles. Born in Milwaukee, Wisconsin, in 1927, he is the expert's expert, and has been writing on career planning for nearly 30 years. It all started in 1970 when he self-published a manual on job hunting titled *What Color is your Parachute?* Every year he updates his 'bible' (and for many job seekers it is just that). Bolles maintains that less than 20 per cent of jobs are found via the internet, and the rest can only be had by getting out there, doing your research and directly approaching those companies most likely to fit your needs, instead of vice versa. Thirty million copies sold is a persuasive reason why you might benefit from his knowledge, either by buying his book or visiting his job-hunting website. The *San Francisco Examiner* calls Richard Bolles 'the most recognized job-hunting authority on the planet' and it's probably right, but the demise of the job and the rise of the work contract mean the process of applying for a full-time job is only one way of getting work.

Dr Peter Carey

Is a career counsellor likely to help me?

For the practitioner, what really matters are the dreams, what will make people happy—and what is in their best interest, not that of their partners, their parents or their bank account.

What is a career counsellor?

There are approximately 3500 counsellors, now more commonly called career development practitioners, in Australia, of whom some 1500 are members of the Career Development Association of Australia (CDAA). These professionals cover a range of career advisory roles in schools, community, corporates, conflict management and resolution and policy development areas.

What do they do?

They work on a one-to-one basis to assist people to take responsibility for their own career development and to become more aware of what the labour market is offering. They deal with people's lives, learning and work. They don't just advise on career change, but also career refinement, including promotion, retirement planning, work-life balance and redundancy.

How do they work?

Many use formal testing instruments to assess your strengths, weaknesses, IQ, EQ (emotional intelligence), as well as interviews in which they discuss your interests, attributes and motivations.

Are they qualified?

There are national standards in place for practitioners. From 2012 new practitioners with the CDAA will need to gain the appropriate qualifications which means, for a professional career development practitioner, a minimum of a postgraduate certificate that has been approved by the industry.

How much do they charge?
Some first visits are free; it depends entirely upon the practitioner. Fees range, on an hourly basis, from $40 for basic schools career advice to $120–$600 for those in private practice. These fees are not currently tax deductible, but the CDAA has represented to government to have this situation reviewed.

How many visits will I need?
That is up to you and your counsellor and the outcome you are trying to achieve.

What if I am unhappy with the service?
There is a code of ethics which governs CDAA members' behaviour and a disciplinary board which handles any complaints.

Dr Peter Carey is former president of the Career Development Association of Australia
<www.cdaa.org.au>

When one size doesn't fit all

Just as the same doctor is unlikely to suit both you and your 92-year-old grandmother, so career practitioners are best selected with care. It is more than appropriate to run through a checklist of questions before settling on which career adviser you might use. After all, this person can potentially help you unlock the mysteries of the universe—your work universe, that is, so it is worth ascertaining if they are on your wavelength and knowledgeable about the sectors which interest you the most.

Some useful questions include:

1. Are you accredited?
2. How long have you been working as a career practitioner?

3. In which areas are you having most success (career change, outplacement, school leavers etc.)?

4. Which types of people have benefited from your support—can you give me some examples?

5. How many sessions will I need to refine my career directions— and approximately how much will this cost?

6. What are the reasonable expected outcomes?

7. And what are not?

And yes, the fees may seem expensive, but then it might be worth asking yourself how much you spent on your last holiday, and if you needed to physically drag yourself back to work because you hate your job so much. If career planning assistance offers an objective environment in which to achieve clarity toward a rewarding career change, then this may be the best money you have ever invested in yourself!

Chapter wrap

The most important connection to make is that between your core values and your labour. Do your career activities nourish your soul? Do you think the work you do is important and of benefit to others? Do your daily activities, both work and leisure, support your idea of living a beneficial life? These are the critical points we need to address before any productive career planning can take place. It doesn't mean we should all rush off and try to emulate Mother Theresa's good work in the slums of Calcutta. It does mean that a basic disconnect between the things we believe are important and the type of work we do is not the recipe for a satisfying life.

Connecting the career dots

Susie Farmer is obviously disappointed she hasn't yet used skills she enjoys, in contrast to Jimmy Pham and Linda White. Jimmy made use of his original 'trade' of travel to revisit his homeland of Vietnam. Here he saw a need and created an informal organisation to offer street children work and the dignity it can bring. With the move to a restaurant, new hospitality skills were required, as was managerial expertise to build KOTO into the successful not-for-profit it has become. Linda has been unafraid of tackling higher education even as a single mother on a reduced income. Her qualifications which allowed her to teach have also meant she is fluent in the language of the country she adores. This fluency enabled her to segue into the travel sector and from working as an employee to running her own business in partnership with another teacher she met through a professional association. Her willingness to continue to train in skills necessary for this business is an important factor in their success.

4

Your work DNA

Up until this point in your life four factors have combined to create a 'work DNA' which sets you apart from the other six billion inhabitants of Planet Earth. These factors are your:

- formal qualifications
- skills
- experience
- achievements

A clearer understanding of our individual work histories offers excellent insights into our possible futures. This chapter contains useful tables which allow you to chart the course you have taken thus far, using this information to identify your future work preferences and opportunities. It concludes with a business-plan-style SWOT analysis (strengths, weaknesses, opportunities, threats) of those attributes of which you can be proud, and those you might wish to enhance as part of your quest for a revitalised career path.

Mapping your work DNA

Deoxyribonucleic acid, or DNA as it is commonly called, stores a set of chemically coded instructions for building and maintaining the structure of living organisms. It is fair to describe DNA as a *unique blueprint* for the creation of an organism. Thus DNA can offer a useful analogy for understanding our own individual work codes. The double helix structure of DNA—with two interwoven strands—also offers a similarly useful framework for understanding how the two different strands of our private and public selves can combine to create a unique work individual. You, as an individual, are the only one who possesses the specific mix of qualifications, skills, and experience which create a pattern that suits particular industries and roles within them.

Your biological DNA is pre-determined—it's all there, coded in the cells of your body. Your work DNA, on the other hand is a particular mix which can *always* be altered and strengthened by the addition of further training, education, experience and exposure to new ways of thinking.

For far too long, too many disgruntled workers have been trapped into believing their work DNA is set once and for all. This is simply not true. Your current work DNA may neatly match requirements for your role as, say, an accountant. Further training, however, may make your work DNA an even better match for another role as, say, a teacher, a year or two down the track.

Let's start by mapping your current work DNA, made up of the four elements listed on the previous page. These elements (which form the *external* strand) when mixed with your interior strand—your values and personality—as identified in Chapter 3, reveal a unique code which sets you apart from everyone else on the planet.

Lisa Shergold:
Gospel-singing bus driver

profile

I left school in Year 10 to study childcare at Box Hill TAFE before working at the Lilydale Childcare Centre for three years. This was followed by a stint as a nanny for four years. I wanted to enter the 'big people's world' so I took a role in customer service in the dispatch department of a tile company. After a couple of years I moved to Australian Gas Light (AGL) where I handled billing enquiries, customer service and trained in various computer programs, eventually being selected for leadership roles. I loved that job and the responsibility of achieving key performance indicators (KPIs). After this I took a couple of sales positions which involved a lot of calls out on the road. There was a lot of freedom and it was good fun. But I got to a point where I needed to reconsider my role. I would put my heart and soul into serving customers and then things would go wrong, particularly in the fulfilment of the sales. I loved being on the road, meeting people and driving but soon lost motivation when I was back in the office.

I was in my early thirties and stuck in a vicious cycle. It felt really wrong.

I asked myself which aspects of the job I loved and the simple answer was, 'Being on the road and meeting people.' One day I was idly looking in a local newspaper and saw an advertisement for bus drivers. I called and was told they wanted more women drivers as they would be gentler on the motors of the buses and might have better people skills. I was accepted for the training and did this in the Dandenong Ranges. But when I was told I had gained my bus driving licence, I panicked. I rang Mum and said, 'What am I doing? A bus driver! This is just silly.'

And Mum said, 'You keep saying you're not happy where you are. You're not going to be in any worse a position if you go and try it.'

I realised we all need to beat the ego thing and be open to different ideas. The Year 12 kids I drive to and from school are never encouraged to think about careers such as bus driving. They're under a lot of pressure to conform to a more professional career plan.

So many people get caught up in the materialistic outer shells and labels. There is a fear factor involved.

The bus I drive is both a community bus and a school bus. I get the kids at the beginning and end of the day and very special older people in the middle. My mum was hospitalised for long periods and I was given love and security by my grandparents. It was this and Mum's love which gave me a lot of empathy for people touched by hardship. The rules may be 'Please don't talk to the driver while the bus is in motion', but the relationships you build with daily passengers are phenomenal. Often I'm the first person they've seen that week. My main obligations are to drive safely, deliver people to where they need to go and to be a trusted friend. The community here is very tight-knit. There's darling Dorrie Dowling who brings me curried egg sandwiches and 70-year-old Peter who brought me a gift, telling me, 'You are like the daughter I never had.' And with the school kids, I just turn up the music and embrace the speed humps!

I will stick with the driving for the foreseeable future. One of my hobbies is as soloist for a gospel choir where we sing very funky, upbeat songs. When the bus is empty, twice a day, I use the microphone and sing out loud. My dad is a pianist. Because my parents split up when I was young, and Dad worked on weekends as a piano player, my brother and I would 'live' under the piano, sometimes falling asleep there. I guess you could say we had notes drummed into us. I also had five lessons in voice when I was about eighteen.

One of my customers on the bus, Clare, has five children, one of whom is a daughter aged seven and a great Pink fan. It got me to thinking about doing concerts for younger kids in the form of a Pink Tribute, but only performing the Pink songs suitable for that age group. I can get my voice close to hers. If I do the Pink shows I may finally be paid for singing professionally. I'm not chasing the almighty dollar, I'm very happy doing what I'm doing 7.30 am to 4.30 pm every day. I've experienced the corporate lifestyle, with a full appointment book, wearing a suit, having a title and a gorgeous car. So many people get caught up in the materialistic outer shells and labels. There is a fear factor involved.

My job is the opposite. There's lots of freedom. You are your own boss, you can build a strong relationship with the passengers—you are really running your own small business. This is bus driving—there are beautiful people out there and I love it.

Lisa Shergold is a bus driver on Victoria's Mornington Peninsula

Identifying *your* work DNA

It's time to identify the elements of your work DNA; to analyse where you have been and what you have done since you were a pimply adolescent walking out of the school grounds, throwing your hat high in the air and shouting, 'Woo hoo, I'm out of here, I'm never going to study again in my life!'

Formal qualifications

Identifying the first element of your work DNA is the easy part. Here *you* recognise *your* secondary and tertiary educational achievements as well as any postgraduate qualifications you have attained (or attempted, but not passed). It's also important to include any other courses, short or long, that you have undertaken. Perhaps first aid, photography, some workplace training, language classes, a responsible service of alcohol (RSA) program, even a driver's licence—any piece of paper, in other words, for which you have trained and been tested—which just might be relevant to some form of future employment. Table 4.1 gives the example of James. Fill in the second row with your own qualifications, noting how James includes *all* training he has received.

Your skills

The second element of your work DNA is the skills you possess. Your skills set you apart from other people who may compete for the same

Table 4.1   Educational qualifications

Secondary	Tertiary	Postgraduate	Other
James McLennan Year 11, Stirling High School 5 subjects in the Leaving Certificate	TAFE Diploma in hospitality	Nil	• Food service • Train the trainer • Introduction to computers • Spanish for beginners • Driver's licence

role. Skills are much harder to define than formal qualifications, as evidenced by the many different skill categories used by government, recruitment specialists and career advisers.

The word 'skill' is derived from *skil*, the Scandinavian word for distinction. A skill can be defined as the ability which comes from knowledge, practice and aptitude and enables you to do something well. Your skills are something you contribute to the world of work, whether the result is a finely tuned piano, a well-pruned azalea, a compelling PowerPoint presentation or a tasty meat pie. Employers will often refer to your 'skill set', meaning the band or collection of skills which equip you to perform well in a defined position. Most of us are apt to underplay our skills, so it is worth taking the time to fill out Table 4.2 comprehensively, describing as fully as possible the group of skills you have gathered during your teens, twenties, and beyond. (You may wish to photocopy the table to make room for all the information you want to include.)

The process of filling out the table might be easier if you relate your skills to the different work projects you have completed since

Table 4.2 Auditing your skills

Year/Age	Role	Tasks	Skills	Skill category*	Experience
Example 1971–1973/19	Clerk— Department of Health	• Cost recording • Reporting against budgets • Manually maintaining spreadsheets • Critical paths	• Following correct procedures • Systems accuracy • Basic numeracy • Ability to work in a team • Ability to meet deadlines	(T), (F) (T) (T) (T), (F) (T), (F)	Some colleagues tried to maximise overtime payments. Our team had to make sure the work was completed during the day so that the wage limits were maintained. This was an eye-opener in how some will abuse the system and how a good manager can encourage others to stop this happening.
Your audit					

*I = industry specific, T = transferable, F = favourite

you first started work—mainly because the various work roles will act as a prompt to recall the many different tasks you performed and have mastered.

The reason for recording all your skills in this table is not to come up with a lengthy and impressive list, but to extract some detail which can then be broken down into one of two categories:

- industry-specific skills (I)
- broader transferable skills (T)
- those you enjoy using the most (F)

Now return to the table to fill in the next to last column with an 'I' or 'T' for *each* skill, and then go back and add an 'F' for favourite in just five of the skills. This should give you a very workable overview of your own particular skill set—as well as a clear idea of those skills which are most personally rewarding, and therefore worth pursuing in your next role. David's example is included to assist.

Your experience

The above listing of your skills in chronological order according to your work experience is a useful element in determining your work DNA. But there's a further element you can identify via your skills listing. Think back to that first job (we'll use the example of an after-school care supervisor). You know the skills you learnt, but what of the experiences gained? Remember the fraught child who suddenly wanted their mother—now!—when she wasn't due until 6 pm? Remember how you soothed the child, contacted the mother and alerted her to the issue but resisted the urge to ask her to collect him early. Or the time two little boys fought over a glass of juice, breaking the glass, and cutting one of their feet? How you automatically used your first aid skills to stem the flow of blood, whilst calming them both down and contacting the school's nurse?

This is the stuff of experience. It may seem small beer now, but at the time it was an important adjunct to the core competencies of organising play, serving oranges and checking the register was signed. It's what you brought to the role. Our working lives offer many extra experiences on a daily basis. Perhaps you work as a landscape gardener. Your skills may involve designing and planning the installation of a water feature on a client's terrace. But your experience may include researching and recommending the installation of a water tank which makes the client's project a responsible and sustainable one. Or maybe you are a human resources manager who was asked at the last moment to present a paper on behalf of your supervisor at a conference in Beijing. This project pushed you far harder than your formal skill set might indicate. From the proofing and editing of the original script to the creation of a visually stimulating PowerPoint presentation, securing online reservations for airfares and accommodation within a pre-determined budget, your ultimate presentation, and the networking and note-taking associated with other speakers at the conference—your experience was worth its weight in gold for your employer. This experience may also prove particularly apposite for future roles and challenges.

So let's reconsider some of the jobs you have had and return to Table 4.2, this time to include some of the experiences you have enjoyed—or endured—across your working life.

Your achievements

Another element of your work DNA is the achievements which come from the application of your skills and nous. Your achievements in the workplace are specific goals attained, projects completed and tasks ticked off. For instance, if we were to return to the example of the after-school supervisor, we could note the organisation of an outing for ten children to the local cinema as an achievement. Yes, this excursion may have used learned skills and provided useful (quotable) experience, but it is also a stand-alone project which was managed and which can be listed as such as evidence for future work. Thinking back over your work and social life, which projects have you undertaken—and pulled off? They may all seem to be work-related, but that would be unusual. There are bound to be family, social and community events which you have also engineered. These achievements are on your 'public' record and well worth considering as part of your work DNA. So take the time now to list three achievements in Table 4.3 (one each relating to work, family and social/community) that demonstrate your ability to tackle a project—and deliver. Again, a sample is provided to help kick-start your thought process.

New directions

You should now have a current and detailed sense of the four 'public' elements of your own unique work DNA. You have noted your qualifications and the work experiences and achievements that have established and consolidated the skills you continue to enjoy using, and those which may be transferable to a new arena. Now it's time to turn from where you have been and open your heart and mind to newer pastures. Let's start by working out which activities motivate you most. This was the thought process adopted by Lisa, the gospel-singing bus driver, when she reached a stalemate in her sales role. Lisa was able to recognise it was the 'on the road' aspect of sales as well as the ability to meet and offer service to a wide range of people that satisfied her the most. The selling and the income weren't particularly strong motivators. What about you?

Work interests and anchors

How do *you* relate to work? Which ways of working thrill you the most? What are your career drivers or motivations? Or, put another way, what gets you out of bed and into the office, the factory, the print shop, the design studio or the bakery each day? There are many ways to define your work motivations. Two of the most useful tools are Edgar Schein's *Career Anchors* and the Harvard Business School mentors, Dr James Waldroop and Dr Timothy Butler's *Business Interest Index*. Both are available on the internet and details are listed in the Notes and Resources section of this book. But be warned, if

Table 4.3 Projects achieved

Project	Type	Tasks involved	Key attributes which contributed to positive result
My mother & father's 60th wedding anniversary—lunch for 40 people	Family	• Guest list • Tracking down old friends • Hiring piano player • Cooking food • Organising drinks • Flowers to replicate Mum's wedding bouquet	Persistence Imagination Creative flair
	Family		
	Work		
	Social or community		

Peter Hatherley:
On being exposed

I'm trying to create a new path. I've given myself a year to make a career out of acting. It's scary. I get opening night jitters and want to die but when I'm on stage I come alive and feel totally engaged with the energy and passion. This year will either end with me in a screaming heap or I might just end up swimming.

When I was at university in the 1970s I did some acting and really enjoyed it. In fact I was close to changing my degree from teaching to arts so I could get into more performance.

But I didn't. I had trained previously as a priest in a Catholic seminary and I didn't know how to tell my parents that I wanted to change again.

After three or four years of teaching I'd had enough, so I moved to the world of advertising, where I ran a financially successful business management consultancy for ten years. We had offices in Melbourne and Sydney as well as overseas agencies. But over time I lost the passion and realised I was just going through the motions. When I first started that business I was fully engaged; you couldn't have stopped me from getting in early. Towards the end, going to the office became a burden not a joy. I was only interested in the end result of making money. So I closed it down.

Following this, there was a time when I felt a bit lost and my marriage eventually broke up. I didn't know what to do, or even what was available. So I used my teaching degree to get by, becoming an emergency teacher. Then I started to work towards doing voiceovers and becoming an actor. I completed a few acting courses with NIDA (National Institute of Dramatic Art) and the VCA (Victorian College of the Arts) and really enjoyed the experience of coming together with people you've never met, and working together, basically becoming a family. This, of course, is the opposite experience to the audition. One I recently attended had about 40 of us reading off against each other. Suddenly I was concentrating more on the others' performances than on my own. It was a bloodbath.

There have been financial and emotional costs along the way. I'm 54 and separated with a teenage son, Josh, who helped me learn my lines before my first break in an amateur play last year. One day he asked if it would be likely I would move back to the large house in which we'd lived in Brighton. I remember pulling the car over to the kerb and saying, 'In my life money has come and money has gone. If you wish to judge me by the amount of money I have, you will see my life as a failure. I choose not to take that as a value guide. You also must make a choice. Whether I am a loser or not—the choice is up to you.' Happily he told me I was 'alive' in the play and that that was a good place for me to be. In effect he gave me permission to pursue this dream.

If you wish to judge me by the amount of money I have, you will see my life as a failure.

In a way performance has been a part of all my careers. As a trainee priest, a teacher and now an actor, I've always had a need to capture an audience and enjoyed the pure drama and theatre of being exposed and making connections. It's definitely allowed me to show off. But there's more to it than that. Particularly with the teaching. As an emergency teacher you have a short window to exert authority over your 'audience' or be run over. It's challenging and, as with acting, there are so many factors you can't control. Every audience brings a different dynamic. You need to know and remain focused on the outcome you wish to deliver.

I'm also conscious of the need to treat my acting ambitions as a business. I need to be in two productions this year. I need to write these goals down and work towards them. I force myself to make at least two contacts a week and expect I will achieve at least two wins, no matter how small, each week.

I pay someone I respect to mentor me. Socrates said a friend should be a mirror, reflecting our greatest good as well as the not-so-good. I depend upon this friend to be upfront about my progress and my performances. Right now I could do with some more acting work and some more wins. I've started so late I'm afraid I'm running out of time to make a difference. But if I have one greater fear it's the possibility I won't give my passion a chance.

Peter Hatherley is an actor and teacher

you choose to use these online tests, you will be required to pay a fee. You can also self-test using the career anchors in Edgar Schein's book of the same name, as you can explore *Business Interest Index* more fully in Waldroop and Butler's book, *Shaping Your Career*. Here is a brief summary of these two different, but equally helpful, ways of understanding what motivates you most in the workplace.

Using career anchors

Edgar Schein was born in 1928, receiving his Masters degree in psychology from Stanford University in 1949. He is considered one of the top thinkers in organisational psychology, partly due to his development of the concept of the eight career anchors which best organise and typify those things people hope to get out of their working lives. These eight anchors are listed and summarised in Table 4.4. It is simple enough to read and select one or two which have the most resonance for you. However to more fully explore your career anchors, you will need to answer a list of 40 'hypotheticals', grading your responses from (1) *Never true for me* to (7) *Always true for me*. The answers to these questions will give a weighting to all eight values, which provides your key anchors

Table 4.4 Defining your career anchors

Edgar Schein's Career Anchors	Career examples	Your strongest anchors	Possible careers
Technical/Functional competence	Electrician	1.	
General Managerial competence	Human resources manager	2.	
Autonomy/Independence	Freelance writer	3.	
Security/Stability	Personal assistant	4.	
Entrepreneurial creativity	Website founder	5.	
Service/Dedication to a cause	Environmental activist	6.	
Pure Challenge	Day trader	7.	
Lifestyle	Personal trainer	8.	

and a clear indication of the important conditions necessary to keep you happy in your work.

This '40-hypotheticals' test can be completed online or by purchasing Schein's book.

Defining your business interests

An alternative assessment tool was developed by Waldroop and Butler from case studies of business professionals at Harvard Business School.

Labelling these preferences as core business interests, Waldroop and Butler have categorised all areas of work endeavour into three main arenas:

- application of expertise
- working with people
- need for control or influence

Table 4.5 outlines the key aspects of these business interests.

Don't let the somewhat formal titles put you off! Take ten or so minutes to underline those examples in the middle column which sound like good ways of earning an income and add other roles to the right-hand column that would appeal to you. This exercise can also help you understand better the type of work which will ultimately prove most satisfying. See how these responses fit with your core values uncovered in Chapter 3.

This exercise can also be more thoroughly explored online or in the book by Butler and Waldroop.

Work environments

The rather broad term 'work environments' can cover a multitude of sins including physical space and psychological climate. Often we think of a work environment as a cultural manifestation, more likely to be associated with large organisations and directly related to the harmony, or lack of, fostered by management. But the work environment is far more complex than the 'fear factor' experienced

Table 4.5 Defining your business interests

Business Interest Type	Specific business interest	Related roles	Roles that appeal to you
Application of Expertise	Application of technology Quantitative analysis Theory development and conceptual thinking Creative production	Software developer Engineer Designer Florist Chef	
Working with people	Counselling and mentoring Managing people and relationships	Psychologist Aged-care nurse Teacher Trainer Nanny	
Need for control and/or influence	Enterprise control Influence through language and ideas	CEO Journalist Minister of religion	

Adapted from Butler & Waldroop, 2008

Professor Barbara Pocock
Designing the do-able job

The most common usage of the term 'work-life balance' suggests a very clever individual sitting on a seesaw holding everything—work, family, community commitments—together with acrobatic ease. This image is placing far too much weight on what we can manage as individuals when what we manage is also dependent upon those we live with, our partners, children and extended families, our social environment our employers and what governments do or fail to do. The external forces have far greater impact on our work-life 'interference' than we do ourselves.

The nature of work is changing dramatically and many workers have significant caring responsibilities which vary during different stages of their lives. Nearly half the workforce is comprised of women. Jobs and households have changed—we now work out of our households. Working from home certain blurs the lines. For some it is a helpful way of avoiding wasted time commuting and they can work more efficiently and coordinate this work with other parts of their lives. Most, however, are dealing with overflow from their day jobs. They use technology to get organised before work or catch up afterwards. It's more often than not unpaid overtime rather than formal occupational support. Computers and mobile phones aren't always weapons of flexibility.

What are the signs that we've lost the necessary balance between work and life?

Sometimes it's a fatal heart attack. Overseas research shows persistent long working hours can cause cardiovascular problems and depression. There are clear health signals when people are wearing out. Other messages include partners leaving or children withdrawing.

It's important to note that most Australians get a lot of pleasure out of their work, with more than half saying they enjoy it. But it's not just about the work—it's often the *terms* of employment that they don't like. Getting a good fit between the hours you wish to work and those in your contract is very important. Some workers are underemployed, but more consider themselves pressed for time. The *Australian Work and Life Index 2009* found two-thirds of full-time workers were often pressed for time. This is not whingeing, it's a serious threat to the health budget bottom line.

Managerial and professional roles are the worst for lack of balance. These jobs are no longer time bound, but task defined. The lack of boundaries for these workers is quite unreasonable. We've always had consultants but now there is a consultant form of employment for workers. The notion of flexibility for portfolio workers is a lot of tosh. Portfolio work usually means someone is working more than they want, are insecure over their life course and often can't respond when friends and family need them. It now takes 1.5 incomes to cover what a single breadwinner delivered a century ago. It is not really possible to live on one normal salary.

Professor Barbara Pocock is Director of the Centre for Work + Life at the University of South Australia

if your boss is a bully or there is an ongoing sense of pressure if all your colleagues arrive early and leave late.

Discerning three different aspects of the work environment helps us to identify further information useful when seeking new or different work. These factors are location, workspace or physical environment, and degree of autonomy.

Location, location

Are you an urban, suburban, regional or rural player? Perhaps you like the bigger stage and describe yourself as a global warrior? Maybe you love the smell of wet concrete and raincoats as you jam yourself onto the 8.04 in downtown Sydney? The tall office towers, the crowds in George Street, uniformly attired in black, grey and navy, an army of brothers- or sisters-in-arms off to do the 'real' business of the day? Or does the sight of yet another traffic jam cause your heart to plummet straight to your boots, and the vision of green fields, or endless plains of golden wheat really set your soul singing?

Recognising the degree to which your work location affects your career satisfaction is not often discussed, but extremely important. We can't all live on a golden beach and enjoy an early morning stroll in the sun before checking in for a day's work. But it may be possible to organise a reasonable commute if you wish to live in one environment, and work in another.

Workspace

Okay, we've located where you will be happiest (and it's not an either/or discussion—it's perfectly fine to note you love working in inner-city Brisbane, and the commute from seaside Caloundra is a small price to pay). But what type of physical environment is going to provide the best workspace for you? Most of us rarely ask ourselves this question—we are so hell-bent on getting that job that the idea of making the physical space a factor in our decision-making seems a little arrogant. It's not. If you are happiest working in a team of one, in your pyjamas, at home or in jeans in a local café, then knowing this can save a lot of heartache before you situate yourself for the next five years in a cubicle in a huge conglomerate in an industrial park which looks like every other industrial park in the country. Consider the jobs you have had and the places associated with those jobs where you felt most comfortable. Maybe it was a library, a supermarket, a crèche, a boardroom, a garage, a kitchen or a catwalk? What did this special space look and feel like? Was it small, intimate, large, open plan? Were there lots of people or few? An abundance of daylight or a phalanx of neon lighting? What does this tell you about yourself? It may be that the core tasks associated with your favourite work were important—but it's just as likely that the physical environment was also one which appealed—and one which will form part of the mix of your next, successful, move.

Autonomy, anyone?

Are you a lone ranger—or a team player? Do you enjoy collaboration with others or are you happier operating on your lonesome? It's been very fashionable recently in corporate land to support the importance of the team—to have ongoing meetings with the team, make decisions as a team, report as a team, and refer to colleagues and team members continually. But maybe that doesn't suit you at all? Maybe you're a crazy professor who happens to enjoy his own company, or a portrait painter who is thrilled at the prospect of long hours perfecting a canvas with just the cat and some classical music for company. Why not? Just because many companies appreciate and value the team players (or say they do), it doesn't mean this has to suit you. And if you are at your best in collaboration with others—does the size of the team have a bearing on your work satisfaction? Maybe like Batman and Robin or Starsky and Hutch you find working as a duo to be great fun? Or perhaps it's the long table and long meeting with twenty or so other bright minds that sparks your creativity? Perhaps you want the best of both worlds— being part of a worldwide team of software developers, online, but working for at least half the time, alone, on a laptop in the back garden? Different strokes for different folks is the rule here, but with how many others do you wish to share the bulk of your working life? The answer to this question offers you a very valuable insight. If you are one of the less collaborative types, it is of vital importance to understand to whom and how often you need to report in any future work assignments. Fill in Table 4.6 to confirm your working environment preferences.

Table 4.6 Working environments

	My best work experience	My worst work experience	What I'm now looking for
Example: Leon Medical student			
Location	University	Supermarket	Academic/research environment
Workspace	Shared laboratory	Checkout	Laboratory
Degree of autonomy	Medium–mainly collaborative work	Nil	Shared responsibility suits me best
Your experience:			
Location			
Workspace			
Degree of autonomy			

Pulling it all together

You've dutifully filled in all the tables in Chapters 3 and 4 and gathered together a lot of information about your inner self and your more public record in the world of work. So how can these insights be used to further your career rethink?

As stated in the Introduction, this review of your work history will enable you to highlight some key crossover points, or repeated patterns which in turn will assist you to identify the most fulfilling aspects of your work so far, and how this knowledge can be applied to find even more satisfying and productive work in the future. The kind of work described in 'Imagine this' in Chapter 1—work that makes you lose all track of time!

Here's one last exercise to help you summarise the insights you have gained from the information gathered so far.

The SWOT analysis

A SWOT analysis is an integral part of most business startup plans. This is how the new business owner analyses and quantifies their business model's strengths, weaknesses, opportunities and threats— hopefully before committing hard-earned savings or investors' capital to a plan that has little chance of succeeding. It's not as commonly used in job search or career change situations which is surprising— for an enterprise of one (you) has just as much at stake.

So let's look at the main questions associated with the four aspects of a SWOT analysis in Table 4.7, and consider them in connection with your work DNA.

There are many different ways of answering each of the questions on the following page. To consider just one aspect—threats—we might feel vulnerable in terms of our age, our industry sector, our physical wellbeing, global financial uncertainty, imports from other countries. In fact, if we put our minds to it, we can feel vulnerable about most things. But this exercise isn't an invitation to commence a negative downward spiral. It is intended to assist you to consider the many positive aspects of your work experience thus far, highlighting

Table 4.7 Your career SWOT analysis

	Formal qualifications	Skills	Experience	Achievements
Strength What makes me competitive in the workplace?				
Weakness What reduces my likelihood of gaining and retaining interesting work?				
Opportunity How can I develop my skills and aptitudes to get even more satisfying work?				
Threat How and where am I vulnerable when considering future work?				

your standout qualities and most important achievements, partnered with a realistic consideration of whether you need to put some work into shoring up those aspects of your skill set which will respond well to training, professional development, coaching, or another form of revitalisation.

A picture emerges

Hopefully by now you will have formed a clearer picture of the things which matter most in your life—and those which matter least, and therefore can be negotiated or compromised. Having considered your main career drivers or anchors, you will have a sense of your preferred work style as well as those roles which may suit you best. And if you have taken time to audit your skills in Table 4.2 you will have reminded yourself of your many skills—and are now excited by the challenge of using them to build a new role. You may also have a far clearer idea of the skills that you might like to enhance in the near future, perhaps even some which you do not currently possess but think could prove worthy additions to those you already have. You have thoroughly identified your work DNA, based on your qualifications, skills, experience and achievements as well as your inner motivation, and now you're ready for one last exercise to help clarify your next steps.

One perfect day

Let's follow the advice of Margaret Goodwin in Chapter 1. Describe in words or, preferably, draw a picture of yourself living your perfect work day. Start with the time you wake, where you are, how you have breakfast, any exercise and social activities, and the work that underpins this day. Make sure your home and location are part of the picture, as well as family, friends, pets and anything else which is very important in your life. Take 5–10 minutes to paint this picture with words or images. Then put it away for 24 hours. When you view this picture again, note the inclusions, the look and feel of where and how you are working and what you are doing. In this image you will find strong clues to what makes you happiest.

Chapter wrap

Remember, change may be inevitable, constant, and unavoidable but it's also PAINFUL! Why does it have to be so hard to find meaningful and satisfying work? The point of steadily working your way through a definition and assessment of your work DNA is not to achieve a quick or easy 'answer', but to spark a conversation. To start a fire in your belly and pique your curiosity to find out more. If I like *this*, then perhaps a fulfilling work project will look like *this*...

Connecting the career dots

The continuing thread in Lisa Shergold's career has been her love of customer service, whether working in childcare, sales, or bus driving. Her role has shifted from new business development to driving and this has required specific skills training. Although she has changed employers and roles she remains happy to work as a full-time employee with defined hours.

Peter Hatherley has taken a bold leap into the unknown by leaving his own company and exposing himself to the 'interview' circuit of castings for voiceovers and acting roles. His education as a teacher stands him in good stead with emergency teaching assignments paying the bills while he tests his new career path. His performance skills from teaching inform his acting and although money is scarce, he has been unafraid to pay for the services of a good mentor to help him keep his career goals on track.

5

What's out there?

Too much choice always leads to confusion. It's no different when it comes to careers. Increasing specialisation has led to a proliferation of employment roles and titles until many of us have little idea of what some—such as change management specialists or cardiac scrub nurses—really mean, let alone what such people actually do. This chapter encourages you to reconsider your future employment options from the perspective of a 'business of one'. It challenges you to rethink potential employment as project-based work opportunities rather than pre-determined 'jobs' for which you will need to apply. This 'Project Hollywood' approach frees you up to consider your search for work using a much more creative framework. In this chapter we look at strategies for this rethink—including taking a sabbatical or time out—as well as the many job possibilities today and in the future and the fastest growing employment sectors where they might be found.

A shift from an emphasis on earning money to enjoying more meaningful pursuits encourages you to reflect deeply on what form your 'cause' might take and the benefits to others that you hope your daily labour will deliver. The aim is to make sure what's out there has a neat fit with what's inside your heart.

A complex landscape

The world of work can be a confusing landscape. When you're flooded with career possibilities, or 'swimming up Niagara Falls', it's good to spend time answering questions like, 'What is the best and highest use of my talents?' and, 'How can I make a bigger impact?'

—William S. Frank, Career Lab

As outlined earlier, unless you have been living under a rock for the past two decades you will be well aware that the world of work is changing rapidly. And that instead of one career we will now have 7.5 or 10.2 or 19.3 careers in a lifetime—whatever that might actually represent. Every day a new type of job is emerging—a job the likes of which we have never known and our grandparents probably could not imagine. It's easy to feel both confused and pressured by the increasing complexity of the world of work.

What will these changes mean—in a practical sense? What type of work is available today and is likely to still need applicants tomorrow?

And, even more importantly, how will these jobs evolve in the future—crystal ball, anyone? What are the new ways of working? Is it getting easier to take a 'gap' year—even if you're closer to 60 than 16? And what of the search for meaning? How do you find work which matches your cause, your political voice, or your civic conscience? Does volunteering mean more than just feeling good? And what about the travel junkies? Can you really find satisfying work which includes life-changing travel experiences? Yes, is the short answer to these questions. But first it is necessary to understand how changes in our 'work contracts' mean we need to adopt a different paradigm for the process of work search; indeed, a recognition that it is up to us to create our own work opportunities rather than seek a job that is waiting to be filled.

'The job' is dead

As we have seen in the previous chapters, there has been, in most sectors, a radical shift in the way Australians work. Put simply, 'the "job" is dead, long live work!' Technically speaking, 'the job' has been on a respirator for many decades, but, as we saw in Chapter 2, the rapid advances in new technologies, in particular, have hastened this demise. ABS statistics show just six million of the ten million working Australians are receiving paid leave entitlements and just 461,000 of those six million workers are on a fixed-term contract. But knowing something intellectually and understanding it emotionally are often two vastly different things. For many, the concept of ongoing employability still comes back to our ability to 'get' a job. It's imperative we discard this historical notion and adjust our thinking to fully optimise our chances of remaining work-relevant.

The two main factors in this workplace change which have direct relevance to a search for new career directions are:

- the work contract (how we are hired and paid)
- the need to remain independent, a direct result of the 'death' of the more conformist company staffer or 'organisation man'

Those who want to remain productively engaged with the workplace for the foreseeable future need to accept these two fundamental concepts.

The contract changes

In *Free Agent Nation: The future of working for yourself*, American author Daniel Pink records the death of the 'organization man'. This term was coined by William H. Whyte in a book of the same name, written in 1956, which described middle-class professional American men working for large companies that demanded, along with professional competence, a high degree of conformity and obedience. In return there would be a job for life. There are many reasons for the decline (if not death) of such a 'man'. Companies seeking to minimise costs and please shareholders have found that it is far cheaper to employ labour on a 'just in time' basis, rather than promise workers a job for life. This has led to an increasing casualisation of the workforce and a cessation of the payment of benefits such as medical insurance. During the past three major economic downturns (1960s, early 1990s and 2008–9), many workers have found that their long years of service have little influence on a manager's decision to retain them. Economic necessity often forces companies to shed more senior workers as this saves the most money.

Large companies have also adopted technology which allows them to become ever more 'remote' from their customers. Gone are the days when a stroll to the high street meant the attention of your friendly bank manager, and a problem sorted. Now it is a long wait on a telephone tree, requiring PIN numbers, passwords and often involving voice recognition 'robots' back-chatting you. It's hard to be loyal to a robot and so the previous 'relationship' between larger companies and real people is further eroded. Companies which choose to hire from a pool of project workers and casuals are now reaping what they sowed in the attitudes of younger workers. Few workers aged below 35 would now take the notion of a job for life seriously, and most would not plan to stay with an organisation for longer than necessary to fulfil their (short-term) aspirations. There is little point in trying to lay blame for the breakdown of the old contract. It's just a reality we all need to factor in.

The individual, not the organization, has become the economy's fundamental unit.
—Daniel Pink, Free Agent Nation

Your business of one

The new concept of payment by output (work project or hourly contractual rate) has led many workers to the conclusion that they need to become a business of one to best represent their own interests when negotiating work assignments.

Daniel Pink has noted this new way of working and has dubbed the United States a 'free agent' nation, a mode which he believes delivers freedom, authenticity, accountability and self-defined success, adding the cautionary note, 'You succeed or fail on your own merits.'

The particular freedoms he notes are not just about place and pace of work, but also the richer sense of ethical freedom, allowing workers to deal with whom they like, in a manner which accords with their most deeply held values. If being a 'free agent' conjures up a picture of a nerdy young man working on a notebook computer in a local coffee shop, that's just part of the story.

Creative workers have tended to be free agents throughout history—wordsmiths, jewellery designers, singers and painters have rarely held down 'day jobs', needing instead to hire out their talents to whoever will pay at the time. But those in more traditional, less overtly creative industries are also finding it necessary to adopt a 'project work' style approach to their careers, with nurses, carpenters, teachers and motor mechanics increasingly forced into seeking assignments rather than long-term appointments. This way of operating doesn't suit everybody. But work is progressively being offered in blocks to those who are flexible enough to work on this basis. Or, to put it another way, as futurist Phil Ruthven notes later in this chapter, our payment is no longer by input (hours per week), but by pre-determined output (completion of project).

Buy it, make it, create it

Does this mean there is a job awaiting your skills and passions, which you will simply slot into, albeit on a project basis?

The other aspect of 'work as project' is that it is no longer a case of an organisation defining an employment need, advertising for a worker, and hiring them. The worker is playing a somewhat passive role in this scenario. Now it is equally likely that the worker will assess what they have to offer, package it and identify a colleague or company which will benefit from their expertise and then 'sell' their skills and experience. The onus has been placed fairly and squarely upon the shoulders of the worker.

There are three broad options in this new world of work. If there is no longer an ongoing 'job' to suit your talents you will need to create one (most commonly by creating your own business and hiring yourself as the most suitable candidate) or to buy one (by investing in an existing business or franchise) or to revamp yourself to match the project work which is currently available in the 'job' market, whilst remaining fully cognisant that this 'revamp' is part of an ongoing exercise—rather like scheduled maintenance on the Sydney Harbour Bridge—for the foreseeable future.

Phil Ruthven
Payment by output

Every industry has a cycle so it is easy to predict the industries which are growing, and declining. Manufacturing peaked at 30 per cent in 1959/60 and is now under 10 per cent. The jobs of the future are growing fastest in the quaternary (information and finance based) and quinary (personal services) sectors with the average household outsourcing at a rate of $24,900 per annum per household. Environment is also a strong theme.

> *People often try to balance work they like, money and status but these three things don't always line up. There will always be a trade-off...*

The way we are paid is changing dramatically and this is better understood by younger generations. The Net generation and Gen X are people who understand being paid by output rather than input. By contrast, Baby Boomers are used to five days per week, nine-to-five and regular holidays. Employers also need to get over the concept of normal working hours. Payment by input NEVER made sense.

Previous working conditions meant people needed to work to a time [set hours]. The days of being paid by input are gone. But the employer and worker need to be able to measure output to strike a reasonable deal.

The ABS reports a trend to work performed at home, or part time from home, part time from the place of work. But when it comes to the notion of 'portfolio' work and working from home full time, these two things are grossly exaggerated. Portfolio work suits a tiny minority of people who have the capacity to handle it. Most people are not good at juggling and don't like it. And work from home can be bloody lonely—even with emails, Skype and the coming holographic technology. People often try to balance work they like, money and status but these three things don't always line up. There will always be a trade-off between money and status and things you like doing.

Phil Ruthven is a futurist who established the online business information company IBISWorld in 1971
<www.ibisworld.com.au>

From money to meaning

The good news about the increasing flexibility surrounding work practices is that when we are forced to rethink our obligation to an employer and to ourselves, an opportunity arises to evaluate the higher needs which our work may be delivering. Put simply, for many workers this involves a very satisfying shift from money to meaning.

In *Transitions: Making sense of life's changes*, William Bridges cites the Buddhist belief that, at a certain stage of our lives, we become ready, willing and able to move into roles which have much more personal meaning than our main career jobs. Social entrepreneurs such as American author and activist, Marc Freedman, think this meaning can be found by engaging in civic ventures. A career trajectory might be understood in two halves. In the first half, when we are lacking strong skills or experience, we tend to find ourselves dancing to someone else's tune. It's logical that amateurs, new recruits and apprentices need to learn the ropes before being allowed to state their conditions in the workplace. Sometimes this results in a total repression of deeply held values and beliefs in order to hold down a job and earn sufficient income to buy the groceries and pay the bills.

Sooner or later, however, it is likely that one of three things will happen.

1. You will arrive in that happy place where you have amassed sufficient wealth and experience to start calling the shots and shaping your career to fit your needs, rather than vice versa. This means you have choices and as long as you are not too comfortable or lazy to change the status quo, it's a pretty good position to be in.

OR

2. You may find that merely being a wage slave isn't enough to feed your soul and you will decide to move to more fulfilling and meaningful work that is much more closely aligned with your values. For this you may need to retrain, or take a significant pay cut, even spend some time out of the workforce considering options and doing the deep thinking that so few people devote to their future. This may not feel quite as comfortable as the first scenario, but it may ultimately prove to be the best move you ever made, giving you long years of true work satisfaction.

OR

3. You may just stay in situ, growing ever more resentful of your role and your 'fate', living a life of quiet desperation where most of your waking hours are devoted to a pursuit which has neither meaning nor relevance to your core beliefs. For this you may even be well paid. But you might also go home every night and dread the fact that the next morning will see you back there at the 'factory' doing something for which you have little empathy and no passion whatsoever.

Only you can judge which scenario fits your current (or planned future) situation. Only you can decide to change this if you're currently enduring option number three.

What does 'meaningful' mean?

Ultimately all work can be described as meaningful as the meaning is bestowed upon it by the worker. Only you can decide if your employment is meaningful to *you*. There are, however, certain characteristics which are common to meaningful pursuits. These are the chance to engage, the opportunity to move beyond the overly repetitive or boring, to be challenged and the ability to do something which will improve the lot of other people, animals or life on earth. Inherent in the term 'meaningful work' there is a lot of scope to find activities that fill us with a sense of satisfaction and the knowledge that what we do really matters.

There are neither easy answers nor water-tight compartments when it comes to defining meaningful work, but the following categories might help you explore your way forward. Your meaningful work might be cause-driven (perhaps political or for community benefit), creative, highly ethical or related to volunteering or cultural travel. In some cases, it could be a mix of all of these qualities—for instance if you were a volunteer for *Médecins Sans Frontières*.

Finding your cause

We are so used to thinking of meaning with a capital 'M' that we often assume there is only one type. Happily that's not the case. There are many types of meaning, and as many causes as people on the planet. In fact, this abundance of options can confuse and swamp those who are hoping to make a difference and leave a legacy. Should you help erect water tanks in African villages, assist dyslexic children to unscramble puzzling word pictures, sing in an acapella group in a nursing home, fight climate change or lobby the local council for more recycling bins? And what if you still need a certain amount of income per week? Is it too much to hope that these tasks might evolve into paid work?

The trick is to explore what 'meaningful' work might mean to you. Which areas of human endeavour strike you as the most useful—and in which of these might your experience, skills and passions be put to best use?

There are any number of inspiring stories of people who have set up huge micro-credit programs, or people such as Bill and Melinda Gates who have invested billions in a charitable foundation. But like the mighty oak, all of these movements and this good work started from an idea—an acorn, if you will. Taking on short-term volunteer projects can help define your longer-term cause.

Becoming a volunteer

Volunteering is an activity in the not-for-profit sector which benefits the community and for which no payment is received. It offers a way to participate in the community, be that local, national or global, and a way to address human, environmental and social needs. A recent ABS survey of voluntary work shows 5.2 million Australians (or 34 per cent of the population aged eighteen or over) participated in voluntary work, donating 713 million hours of their time in a twelve-month period. The pattern of volunteering varied with life stage; parents with dependent/school-age children being the most likely to give their time. The four most common types of volunteering, accounting for 75 per cent of activity, were sport and physical recreation, education and training, community/welfare and religious. Emergency services is also an important category, with 175,000 Australians giving 26 million hours per annum to this cause.

The two-way street

Is volunteering right for you?

Even more importantly, are you right for it?

Tim Spurdens:
The impossible job

In 2003 I moved to the Kanpi (pronounced *Gumpi*), a small Aboriginal community on the Anangu Pitjantjatjara lands (APY Lands) located six hours by road south-west of Alice Springs. I had previously experienced volunteer work in Laos as an English teacher when my wife, Doreen, went there to work for Australian Volunteers International. Although it was my toughest work assignment in a career spanning nearly 50 years, I would also describe it as a time of great growth.

I knew it would be a full-on 24/7 position before I accepted. After our volunteer experience in Laos I was seeking similar work, but in our own country. I found an advert for this position in the local paper. I had to travel to Kanpi to see the community and have a 'meet' for approval—although only three people turned up. There are twelve houses there and a floating population of about 50 to 80. They don't have a lot of interest in running the place although Marita, the Chairperson, is about as good as you could get. The role was as a Municipal Services Officer (MSO, similar to a CEO in an urban shire or council). The major problems in the community stemmed from the fact that there was no real work available. Most residents received CDEP (Community Development Employment Projects) cash fortnightly delivered on the plane from Alice Springs to the local airstrip.

It proved to be an impossible position in which to make progress. Typically you would want to go into a place and improve things . . . but you don't. I lasted two years but was ragged at the end of it. It was previously run by Mick, a very experienced storeman. He couldn't handle it, either. The theory is that the town council employs the MSO and gives instructions. The practice is that the MSO just does everything. It's a potentially fabulous position, but impossible to make progress. The first step would be to get some employment there. I had the idea of creating a date plantation, utilising underground water supplies and funding from government bodies. But I just couldn't get it going. The senior men had enjoyed work on missions and cattle stations much earlier in their lives. But when it became law that payment, and not just board, was required these jobs fell away.

Over the two years I learnt to become much more tolerant. I'm not normally an aggressive person, but the locals would wind me up, telling me I was on their land so why should I think I could tell them what to do? So I would argue back. It took me a while to learn not to. Doreen visited a few times during the two years and I had a week's leave every three months which I normally took in Alice. Apart from this, I felt pretty isolated out there with no support except for Mick in the store. By the time I left I just couldn't handle it anymore. I didn't do anything for a few months, I was so burnt out. But then I visited the Volunteering SA website, seeking an indigenous program in Adelaide.

I now work in financial counselling for the Aboriginal Legal Rights Movement, a support program for those on low incomes. I am paid for my work on Tuesdays but give an equal amount of time, gratis, on Wednesdays. It's for people who have trouble managing money—maybe too many bills, threats of service disconnection, maybe something to do with their superannuation. We see a lot of disability pensioners and people from the local prison who need public housing. Again, it's tough work but rewarding. We get lots of hugs and thanks. And it seems to be leading me into different work opportunities including ways to put pressure on governments to recognise and address the shortage of affordable housing for indigenous people.

Life is so interesting and varied. My recent work is most definitely not about the money. Even if you only do it for a few years it can stand you in good stead and can help you gain other employment.

For me, volunteering has been a hugely beneficial experience which has kept me employment-relevant by keeping my brain moving and stretching my interests far beyond bike riding and playing tennis. It is so important to have greater meaning in your life and to feel you are doing something useful rather than becoming a blob.

Tim Spurdens is a volunteer and financial counsellor

It is easy to see the benefits of volunteering—in fact, it's a no-brainer. Volunteering allows us to work for a cause that interests us and we consider worthwhile. It also affords us the opportunity to make a difference, create change, build new skills, meet new people and add variety to our paid work experiences. For many people, including Tim Spurdens, volunteering has also provided a stepping stone to a new career direction.

But whilst it may seem obvious that to engage in a volunteering opportunity will enhance your future work prospects, it's not just about you. It's imperative to understand that not all organisations are waiting impatiently for you to grace them with your presence and talents. In fact, you may be totally unsuited to many positions within the not-for-profit sector. How do you find this out before committing time and energy to the wrong cause? By defining the type of volunteering you would like to do and then approaching the volunteer coordinator within this organisation to ask about the qualities they consider most important in the people who donate their time.

With 700,000 listed not-for-profits in Australia, the opportunities for using your skills and energy as a volunteer are far too numerous to canvass here. There are many excellent websites that cater to those wishing to explore the type of projects to which they are suited. Some are listed in the Notes and Resources section at the end of this book.

Travel junkies

Travel junkies thrive on dislocation. When they seek new career options they often aren't seeking a new type of work at all. Instead they are looking for a new direction a long way from where they currently live, often in a much more challenging culture. This can sometimes be achieved by those working in a large enough enterprise, by requesting a transfer and becoming an expatriate. Others have found volunteering with organisations such as Australian Volunteers International a great way to secure short- and long-term offshore assignments.

In fact, there are so many ways of working away from home, be it interstate or overseas, that the range of choices can overwhelm. Start by considering your primary reason for seeking a travel-focused change. Is it driven by your desire to live elsewhere—or are you just in need of a good holiday? Understanding the difference is critical. We've all been victim to great 'expat lit' which describes the joys of the small town in Provence—and skims over the detail of the adverse weather, low employment opportunities and tough visa regulations for those who need to draw an income. Other questions to consider are the portion of your current salary you hope to maintain, and how long you would be happy to be away. How far you wish to go, for how long and how this might affect the family are equally important considerations. So is the size of your savings account—do you have sufficient money if things go pear-shaped? And if there is a significant other in your life, are they happy to travel with you—or just as happy to let you go? If your travel stars are aligned, and the above questions present no major problems, start your planning by looking at Lonely Planet's *The Big Trip: Your Ultimate guide to gap years and overseas adventures*. Yes, it's primarily written for the under-30 age group but there's no reason why older adults can't get excited by a gap year as well!

Occupation shopping

Society seems fairly forgiving of school leavers who don't know what they want to do, so their propensity to pick a tertiary course and drop out is generally well accepted. There is also an army of people who try to support teenagers grappling with career choices and a general understanding that they might not get it right the first time.

Not so with adults. We are all meant, somehow, to not only know where we are going, but also how long it will take us to get there. For those aged from 20 to 90 who have absolutely no idea what they want to do when they 'grow up', this is rather depressing. If only we could all head back to the comfort of the (free-of-charge) vocational guidance teacher, someone whose role was to spend their time guiding us through the pathways to the perfect career!

Given that we can't go back—and there is no such thing as a perfect career, anyway—it's up to us to initiate our own career shopping spree.

First stop, the *Job Guide*

The longer we have held the same job, the more difficult it becomes to even imagine new and different types of work which might inspire and engage us. But there is help at hand!

In April each year the Federal Government Department of Education, Employment and Workplace Relations (DEEWR) sends every school a copy of the *Job Guide* for each Year 10 student. This is a fabulous tool which helps students start to think about their future work possibilities. The really good news is that this list of 1500 occupations and specialisations is also available online (see the Notes and Resources section for web address). All occupations are sorted alphabetically, although searches can also be done using job titles and keywords. Each job title is accompanied by a job description, a list of related tasks, specialisations, related jobs and education and training and employment opportunities on a state-by-state basis.

Why reinvent the wheel? If you think you may be interested in a particular role, visit the *Job Guide* website to gain an up-to-date overview of the type of work you would do in that role, other associated career opportunities and the type of training and qualifications you may need to succeed.

Another way of using this website is to enter your current role and note the specialisations and related jobs. Maybe one of these will provide the segue you have been seeking—at the very least it will probably help crystallise your thinking about the work you currently do, the aspects which you enjoy, and those you would rather leave behind.

The big picture

But seeking information on specific jobs is perhaps missing the wood for the trees. Individual jobs which exist today are only part of the fabric of the world of work. Consider the existing jobs as the thread—it is the weaving of weft and warp which creates the cloth, and the major strands can be viewed as industry and sector groups. Some sectors and industries are emerging while others are on the wane.

Depending upon which statistics you choose to read, the Australian workforce is composed of five main sectors, broken down into about eighteen industry profiles. In Chapter 1 we considered the inexorable movement of workers from primary to secondary, to tertiary industries. We are now witnessing a major shift into the quaternary and quinary industry groups (see Table 5.1), resulting in an increase in work opportunities for knowledge workers.

How does this macro view affect individuals? Should we let the big picture influence our job selection? If we are interested in roof thatching, an honourable task, centuries old, why, if our first love is to thatch, should we care if jobs in primary industries are down to 5 per cent? The short answer is no, you don't necessarily have to renounce ambitions for a career in a 'sunset' industry, but it is important to be aware that that future employment prospects may be tight and to factor this into your career thinking.

A top-down view of working Australia

As noted, the Australian economy can be broken down into five industry sectors; primary, secondary, tertiary, quaternary and quinary. Table 5.1 shows activities associated with each of the sectors, and the

2007–8 percentage employment and contribution to Gross Domestic Product (GDP).

As Phil Ruthven has noted, every industry has a cycle and it is easy to predict those industries which are growing and those which are declining. The agricultural sector peaked as an employer in the 1840s, making a 50 per cent contribution to GDP. It now contributes just 2.5 per cent and the percentage of workers employed is almost the same, approximately 3 per cent. Manufacturing peaked with a 30 per cent contribution to GDP in 1959/60. This is now down below 10 per cent, and employment represents 10.3 per cent of the population.

Future growth

Unsurprisingly, the greatest growth is occurring in the quaternary and quinary sectors. One of the major contributors to the job spurt in the quaternary sector is the communications industry which, with new technologies being developed every day, is requiring an army of workers to deliver and service them. Information and finance also remain strong, long-term areas. The quinary sector includes services created to satisfy the demands of household outsourcing, calculated to be worth $24,900 per annum per family. Even during a severe economic slowdown, Phil Ruthven predicts this services sector will continue to grow: 'Original outsourcing was when we moved from growing food in the backyard, building our own homes, making our clothes and furniture and preserving food. When homes and businesses start to outsource, new businesses and industries are created. Businesses no longer own trucks or run canteens. Outsourcing may take a temporary hit—but few will buy a $500 mower and replace their mower man. Most people won't stop outsourcing—either they don't know how to do it, or have made a value judgement that they cherish the freedom they have "bought". Old skills may be learned as a hobby or therapy but not because of need. We won't go back to raising chooks in the backyard.'

Another area of activity which seems set for significant growth in numbers employed is the Aged Care sector—bound to boom when

Table 5.1 Australian jobs 2008			
Industry sector	Industry profile	% contribution to GDP	% employed
Primary	Agriculture	2.4	3.5
	Mining	7.7	1.5
Secondary	Manufacturing	9.9	10.3
	Construction	7.1	9.1
	Utilities	2.0	0.9
Tertiary (commerce)	Retailing	5.4	14.4
	Wholesaling	4.5	4.6
	Transport	4.7	4.7
Quaternary (information & finance)	Property/business services Education	12.2	11.7
	Government	4.0	7.5
	Finance & insurance	3.8	4.4
	Communications	7.4	3.8
		2.4	1.7
Quinary	Health	5.8	10.4
	Hospitality	1.9	4.9
	Personal services (household outsourcing)	1.8	3.9
	Cultural & recreation services	1.5	2.6

Compiled from data on *Australian Jobs 2008* website

the demographic peak caused by the baby boom of the 1950s and 1960s starts to age.

Fastest growing industry themes

According to Phil Ruthven, the following areas of activity are experiencing growth. These work trends have emerged since the mid-1960s and are predicted by IBISWorld to continue to feature strongly through to the 2040s. It is not surprising to see information communication and technology head the list, but other growth industries will also require a strong understanding of technology. The trend to outsource home services remains robust, with outsourcing of educational services also tipped to increase. 'Green collar' jobs will increase with industries based on sustainable practices and measurements beginning to emerge. Those interested in remaining employment relevant should be aware of, and responsive to, these growth industries.

New Age 1965–2040s

- Information, communication and technology (ICT)—the New Age all-pervasive utility
- Business services—outsourcing non-core functions
- Financial services—outsourcing of transactions/investment
- Property services—outsourcing property ownership or services
- Knowledge industries—databases and multimedia services
- Health—outsourcing home doctoring
- Education—outsourcing pre-school, plus universities
- Personal and household services—outsourcing chores
- Hospitality and tourism—outsourcing the kitchen and travel needs
- Recreation and cultural services—outsourcing leisure
- Mining—energy minerals (oil, gas, coal, uranium)
- Biotechnology and nanotechnology—New Age technologies

Career shopping, Part Two

As well as the *Job Guide*, each year the Australian Government releases an overview entitled *Australian Jobs* which includes a prediction of jobs growth for the next five years. This handy document is available by download from the Department of Employment, Education and Workplace Relations website (listed in the Notes and Resources section). The seventeen listed industries are not the same as those used by IBISWorld, but have a close correlation. Table 5.2 lists the top ten industries for employment growth as predicted in *Australian Jobs 2008*, as well as the anticipated amount of growth. These predictions were finalised before September 2008 when the global financial downturn first manifested itself. The effect of the downturn on specific industry employment statistics is yet to be revealed.

The *Australian Jobs* report offers a very clear and current summary of these industries and occupations with employment prospects and likely salaries. This provides a very useful tool for anyone who is career shopping.

Table 5.2 Australian jobs 2008–predicted growth			
Industry sector	% anticipated increase by 2012-13	% aged 45 years or older (all industries average = 37%)	% outside capital cities (all industries average = 37%)
Health & community services	19	46	37
Property & business services	19	37	27
Retail trade	16	26	38
Construction	13	33	41
Education	9	49	38
Accommodation, cafés & restaurants	5	26	43
Transport & storage	5	44	33
Government administration & defence	4	45	37
Cultural & recreational services	4	32	34
Mining	15	34	63
Other	6		

Complied from data on *Australian Jobs 2008* website

The need to reflect

It's hard to see clearly with sweat in your eyes.

—Anon

Reflection is not a highly prized quality in today's fast-moving world. We seem to have lost the ability to sit back and quietly think through our sense of what is important. Our best thinking rarely occurs at six in the evening after a hard day on the tools, keyboard, or road.

Our most creative thoughts, instead, are usually those free to rise when we are feeling rested, refreshed, and full of the possibilities of human existence. More importantly, our most insightful thoughts are only possible when we remove our current work blinkers and allow ourselves the luxury of dreams without limitations. Sure, at some time you may have to get practical and realise, at 52, it is highly unlikely you will rival Roger Federer at Wimbledon. But if the sporting world is your passion and delight and your talents lie in the areas of promotion or finance, who says these skills can't be nurtured to allow you to work in the world of tennis?

Gotta go

Getting away from your current day job may be difficult. If you also juggle another job, family or carer obligations or other important commitments, it may seem impossible. But if the alternative means you are doomed to remain in a role which is less than satisfying and the likelihood is that you will become evermore frustrated or disheartened, then where is the choice? Somehow, whether it means bartering money, your time, or your skills, you will need to arrange some time out from your ongoing duties to allow you to reflect.

The point of this reflection time is to loosen your grip on the present in order to create a vision for your future.

It may be unrealistic to expect such a process to occur within a weekend, but a visit to the country or coast usually presents the perfect natural setting in which a 'blank slate' for our future can be imagined. Others may achieve this same effect from mental time out using meditation or other relaxation techniques, but leaving the scene of the crime (i.e. your workplace) is usually the best way to go.

The case for a sabbatical

What if you could run away, not just for a couple of days, but for a much longer period of time? Financial constraints mean the sabbatical is a luxury denied to most of us. And even if we might afford twelve months away from paid work, ongoing commitments to family and work colleagues will normally scupper that particular plan. But let's at least explore the possibility of a sabbatical, a break normally associated with universities which grant academics extended leave to take stock, learn more, and return refreshed to their roles.

So what stops us?

It tends to come down to two things. First, the belief that our employer will not hold our job for six months or a year and that we will need to resign and therefore give away our (perceived) job security. Second, that we simply cannot afford to continue to pay our mortgage and household expenses while having time off work. And yes, for those who are on a limited income, or a high income, but highly geared, this is most probably true. But if you don't want to burn your bridges in your current work situation, let's explore how you might counter these two very real obstacles.

The average life span of an Australian male is 78 years, and a female can look forward to 82 years. Given that this is an average, and that it is becoming increasingly normal to know a centenarian, those who start work at 18 or 20 or 22 and work through to the Age Pension–defined retirement age of 65 (rising to 67 in 2023) will spend more than 40 years of their life working between 40 and 60 hours a week with a break of just four weeks a year—enough time to collapse in an exhausted heap at a beach, with a multitude of other workers lying similarly prone. An annual holiday might provide a rest, but it's hardly mental, physical or spiritual rejuvenation.

Putting your job on hold

If you do want to return to your current position after time out, then, before you commence negotiations with your manager or employer, it's worth realising that this is a huge bonus for your organisation. The cost of recruiting, retaining and rewarding good staff is high. The cost of replacing them when they leave, taking years of company knowledge with them, is even higher. If you are delivering value in the workplace *it is highly likely your employer will move mountains to keep you happy*. Two things to summarise—if you don't ask for some time out you won't get it—and you are probably far more valuable than you ever considered.

What about the money?

Tackling the need to finance a sabbatical is not quite so straightforward, but it *is* probably more affordable than first thoughts indicate. If you are the breadwinner for a family with a stay-at-home mum or dad, and very young children, servicing a huge mortgage and barely covering household bills and food, then yes, this is too great a leap of the imagination. If, however, you are under financial pressure because you spend too much on consumer goods you don't really need, there is definitely some room to move. Let's assume you would like six months' leave. Let's also assume one month will be covered by holiday pay and that you are planning for this time off twelve months in advance. Start today, by creating an automatic deposit of one-eleventh of your monthly salary in a lockup cash account, *before* you receive the balance. Yes, it will be tough. Yes, you may be tempted to over-use your credit card to compensate for the lack of cash. And if you do, you'll be able, at the end of twelve months, to withdraw your savings and pay it off, as well as the horrendous accrued interest. But if you are vigilant and determined, you will have the money to fund extended leave, and that excuse will be gone.

You might even have to see your boss and go through with it!

Don't expect answers

You will not necessarily walk away from your time out or sabbatical with answers—in an ongoing career journey there are no definitive answers, just better questions to ask. What you may also do is spark a conversation with yourself, one which offers new thoughts and insights and which, hopefully, is ongoing.

Donny Morrison:
If not now, then never

profile

I've been teaching English as a foreign language in Hanoi for six months now. Before that, I was living in Scotland and working for the Scottish Environment Protection Agency (SEPA) since 1996. I was very happy with this organisation . . . and I was also happily married. But then last year, my marriage unexpectedly ended and, over a period of time, I realised I would benefit from a new challenge in a new environment. Turning the Big 40 last August was also a factor!

My first job was washing dishes at Wimbledon Tennis Champion-ships, twenty years ago! My first degree was Electronics Engineering, at Glasgow University. I disliked the degree very much but stuck it out because I wasn't sure what else to do. Within two years of graduating, I took an MSc in something completely different—Marine Environmental Protection. This then led to my job with SEPA. So, I suppose in some ways I had already started over again.

The single most important thing I've learnt about work is to always try and be as helpful and polite as possible with people you work with. There may well come a time when you need their help.

SEPA is a government organisation and, as such, employees are entitled to ask for a sabbatical of up to two years. This is not a 'right' and much depends on the support of your line manager. I was fortunate to have a very supportive line manager who made the whole process of arranging a sabbatical very easy for me. I asked for (and was granted) just fifteen months as I had genuine concerns that I would be homesick and/or not find suitable employment. I decided that teaching English would be a good way to spend my time abroad, and so I took a four-week course (CELTA qualification) before I left Scotland. I spoke to friends who have taught English abroad, friends who have travelled in Asia and I consulted lots of websites and books.

With every month in Hanoi, I have felt more and more settled both in my teaching job and also with living in the city itself. So, in May I asked SEPA if my sabbatical could be extended by another nine months, giving me two years all up. Happily they approved my extension so I am not due back in Scotland until October 2010.

A typical day involves some lesson preparations at home in the morning and then meeting friends for lunch or coffee. I start teaching at around 3 pm, and finish around 9 pm. I teach both children and adults in one of the biggest private English schools in Hanoi. I am thoroughly enjoying my teaching. It still feels 'new' to me, I feel that I am learning new things all of the time and I feel very invigorated. This was an absolute step into the unknown for me (part of the attraction!), so I had no idea what to expect. But, by the same token, I felt last year that if I don't do it now, I never will. My marriage ended, I don't have any children and therefore it was a time when my lack of responsibilities and ties afforded me an opportunity to do something different. If I was to be honest, in the run-up to starting my sabbatical, I did have moments when I thought, What on earth am I doing?

While I am naturally a (quietly) confident person, my confidence was affected by the upheaval in my personal life last year. To help regain this, I came to the view that it would be good for me to completely step out of my comfort zone. This was daunting, and a big challenge. But it has worked out very, very well and I can honestly say that I am happy and content. My 'goal' is being achieved.

I have taken a salary cut but the cost of living in Hanoi is so low that I am actually better off! My plan is to return to SEPA and then work until I am 60. However, the thought of doing nothing in retirement terrifies me. I like to keep active. I now feel that, as I am a qualified and experienced teacher, this is something that I may return to at some point. But one thing last year taught me is that you can never know what is around the corner.

Donny Morrison is a volunteer and English language teacher

Conditions will never be right

What came first—the chicken or the egg?

This is an age-old conundrum which we know we'll never solve.

Similarly, it is often difficult to separate the cause and the effect when it comes to the earning of income and enjoyment of meaningful work. Should we work like stink at a job we don't like that much because that is the job which suits our qualifications and the one for which we will receive the highest remuneration?

And when we have 'made it', can we then relax, enjoy a degree of choice, and move into work which satisfies our soul and rewards our desire for more freedom or better work–life balance?

Or should we start by seeking more satisfying work, and allow ourselves a pre-determined period of time to live off the (presumably) lower income and adjust our material needs down to this income, thus immediately satisfying our need for meaning?

It's a question worth pondering—and you won't be the first. Many of us want to make changes to our working lives, but are waiting for the conditions to be right.

Sadly, this will never happen through waiting.

No matter which new challenge we face, the conditions will never be absolutely right to get started.

At some stage we need to recognise that trade-offs are inherent in all employment choices. *Some* of the conditions may be able to be changed, but if you are waiting for the perfect moment to seize control of your destiny, *when* the kids have grown up, *when* the kids have left home, *when* you have enough money, *when* you are offered the redundancy package, *when* an interesting job is advertised, then you really are dreaming. Some of these things may indeed happen in the future—but by then you will have come up with a brand new condition (read excuse) that needs to be met, once again, before you are ready to change.

Sadly, the conditions will *never* be completely right to change from an unsatisfying role. You will need to find the courage to make that change regardless. Or cope with staying put.

Chapter wrap

What matters most? That there are more work options but too much choice often only serves to confuse.

The message in this chapter is the importance of taking time to reflect upon the work you believe is both meaningful and capable of offering a sustainable career path. Arm yourself with the aforementioned occupational 'catalogues' so you have some objective and current information on the types of work that are available, and understand that waiting to make a move until the conditions are perfect and you've 'made it' is akin to waiting for hell to freeze over.

Connecting the career dots

Tim Spurdens changed his way of working in every category on the career dot grid. In particular, a radical change in location to the remote APY lands saw him working, largely unsupported, in a new role, and a very different culture. The volunteering stint in Laos provided a partial preparation but culture shock still prevailed. His current role highlights the possibilities of volunteering as a pathway to future work projects.

Donny Morrison also stepped into the unknown but is using his sabbatical to experience something different with the security of a job he enjoys to return to. He needed to take on new skills, the UK equivalent of the Teaching English as a Second Language (TESL) certificate to make this change happen. His gamble has worked and he has now chosen to extend his time out to further stretch his Vietnamese adventure.

6

Planning your next move

Now it's time to move into some serious career transition planning. This transition might simply involve an adjustment of working hours and location; more time telecommuting and less time spent in traffic jams, resulting in more free time to spend on a favourite hobby. Or you may be seeking a more radical change. This chapter considers the career segue, revisiting the 'Connect your career dots' system introduced in Chapter 1, to allow you to plot your course, consider new areas of activity and ways you can gain entry to the type of work you would much prefer to be doing. Rather than simply considering the 'theory' of career change you are encouraged to do some work and fill in the tables as you read so you will have a clear, measurable and achievable set of tasks; the first step toward achieving positive career changes. Your goal could be to retain your current role, but to renegotiate it to better suit your values and interests. If so, you will enjoy learning how to pitch your plan to your current employers and tackle any potential obstacles along the way.

Get on with it

You've found your passion, but how do you shape this into a purposeful role that is both realistic and achievable?

Although it is impossible to plan your entire lifetime career path—and who would really want to?—you can dramatically shape your next move. You can't plan your whole career path because the job you will be doing in ten years' time probably doesn't exist yet. This may sound like bad news for those with a yen for long-term planning. But it's great news for those of us who procrastinate or yearn for the conditions to be perfect before we make our next move. As we have seen, the conditions will never be absolutely right—and we cannot accurately predict the shape of future jobs—so now it's time to just get on with it.

First, let go

One of the reasons you may find it difficult to stop thinking and start to act is that you may not be psychologically prepared to farewell your past or your current working role. You may be intellectually committed to a new path, but perhaps this commitment is only skin-deep and, in your heart of hearts, you just can't let go of old ways.

Many psychologists have written about the sense of grief and loss when something is taken from us. At the deepest level this might be the loss of a loved one, or a way of life (as a political refugee might experience). It seems shallow, by comparison, to be caught in the grief trap for something relatively less important, such as our work. But whether or not it seems trivial on the scale of human misery, so much of our sense of self and self-esteem is tied up in the work we do that it would be strange not to mourn the passing of a significant work role. William Bridges notes this grief in his book *Transitions* when he talks about the need to first let go: 'To become something else, you have to stop being what you are now; to start doing things a new way, you have to end the way you are doing them now; and to develop a new attitude or outlook, you have to let go of the old one you have now.'

Put more simply, it's back to the old adage that if you keep doing things the same way, you'll get the same results. Very few human beings are capable of embracing change wholeheartedly. But if we want to improve our working lives—*and are unsatisfied with our current situation*—then there is no choice but to make a move.

Ella James:
It's not the mistake

I love Mark Twain's notion to let your 'vocation be your vacation'. It's important to find your heart's desire, then find someone who will pay you to do it.

My first job was in the 1970s working for my mother's law stationery business. I licked stamps for envelopes while I watched *Mr Ed* after school. I was nine. But I've really been an entertainer all my life, just paid for it for the past eight years.

I love what I do, every part of it, every moment of it . . . even the waking up unemployed every day until a booking comes in!

I would have liked to work in musical theatre. Like most single parents, my mother was forced to make a decision when I was younger: either take my sister and me to swimming, or let us learn ballet. My sister had two left feet and it was decided I would benefit from swimming . . . so ballet was dropped. I think if I had learnt music, singing and acting, my life would have been very different, although having said that, I have no regrets, I am happy to work as a speaker, comedienne and voiceover artist, and am amazed that it has turned out this way.

It took a lot of courage to change. I had worked in radio for twenty years, and had success in it, but always felt something was missing . . . when I finally got in front of a live audience, it was as though something clicked into place. The courage came in the form of me having to believe in myself; believe that I had something to offer audiences as myself, rather than being a conduit for information through news and talkback.

I sought advice from everyone I could. I was honest in my questions and where I was at, at the time. I found some extraordinarily helpful and supportive people, in particular Diana Mann, at ICMI Speakers Bureau, offered advice, encouragement and support and is now a valued friend.

I hope to always be doing something similar and have started mentoring others in their careers. I teach at AFTRS (the Australian Film, Television and Radio School) and MEAA (the Media Entertainment and Arts Alliance) advising people on a career in voiceover.

... it's important not to get stuck in well-intentioned conversations with people who encourage victimology.

I've been retrenched once and fired thirteen times, most recently by 2UE in 2005.

I received a call from the Station Manager's PA on Melbourne Cup Day asking me to come in for a meeting the following day. I immediately 'knew' that this wasn't good. I rang my late mother, who was in a nursing home at that stage, and burst into tears . . . it was a 'not again' scenario . . . after all, it was number thirteen! I will never forget her saying, 'Oh for heaven's sake, you speak to corporate audiences about happiness and being positive. They might want you for something wonderful!'

So, I walked into the meeting joyful and hopeful, and had actually talked myself into thinking they wanted me to fill in for John Laws or something similar over the Christmas break. When they told me they had replaced me and there was nothing more for me at the station, I was quite angry and said, 'You mean you are prepared to let me go?'

Ego or self-belief? Not sure, ha ha!

Anyway, the box of tissues came out from under the desk and I had a cry and the program director rang me the next day and told me what a fabulous talent I was. But it was then that I made the decision to focus entirely on my speaking and voiceover career. Since then, I have started acting classes and have also done stand-up comedy, making it into the Sydney finals of the Raw Comedy Festival, part of the International Comedy Festival in Melbourne. A wonderful journalist I worked with in the early 1980s, Les Thompson, once told me, 'It's not the mistake, it's the recovery.' He was talking about making a mistake in a news bulletin, but I have extrapolated it to life. I think it's a good plan.

I believe it's important not to get stuck in well-intentioned conversations with people who encourage victimology. It's happened, it's over. Mix with people who are positive and ask them what qualities and skills *they* see you having that perhaps you haven't seen in yourself. Life is multi-faceted, like a diamond. You might have only been looking at one facet, but in order to shine, you need to turn the diamond around and see it from different angles. Be kind to yourself, get lots of sleep . . . start each day with a walk, and as Mum used to say, 'Don't worry about money. If you're going to worry about something, worry about something important.'

Every time I get in front of an audience, I hope to do my best performance yet. And I know what it will look like—a room full of smiling people.

Ella James is a broadcaster, speaker, MC and voiceover artist <www.ellajames.com.au>

Small steps, big rewards

How much of your life do you devote to planning? Most people don't take career planning seriously unless it is imposed externally—normally by an employer. Often it is associated with the grief of job loss—as part of an outplacement exercise offered out of benevolence, good practice or guilt, by someone who just sacked you. Not perhaps the best time to look optimistically at your future work opportunities. As with most other things in life, it is important to get on your front foot here if you can, and do your own career planning well in advance of that sanctioned by others. This involves a four-step process:

1. a 48-hour break to open your mind
2. an understanding of how career moves are made
3. a comparative imagining of two viable alternatives
4. some goal- and deadline-setting

48 hours

How much time does the next five or ten years of your life deserve? If you get the next move right, you will earn a fair wage for interesting work which will help you grow as an individual. What is this worth to you?

It's amazing how often we are prepared to drop everything for a family member or a friend in need, and how lightly we value our own needs. It is a well-known strategy when encouraging people to adhere to a new fitness routine to suggest they make a date with a buddy. Not because the buddy needs a workout, nor to turn the fitness schedule into a social outing. But because nearly all of us will crawl over hot coals before letting down a friend.

When it comes to committing a sizeable whack of time to yourself, all this loyalty and support seems to evaporate. There is time to drive 300 kilometres to watch your daughter's netball team, time to help a friend move house, time to watch the final of *MasterChef* and see Julie secure a satisfying work future. But there appears to be a drastic shortage of time to devote to your own future work happiness. Again, the brutal truth is that you will need to get over this attitude to make any worthwhile forward progress.

Decide now which weekend in the next month you will devote to your career segue.

Mark it in the diary, and if at all possible, beg, borrow or steal accommodation where you can do your private thinking. This invokes the no partner/spouse/best buddy rule as well. As much fun as it is to share this important time, this is about you and you alone. It's not often we get the chance to be totally introspective, so make it happen at least this once. The funny thing is, you'll probably find it such a fulfilling exercise, that you will want to make this a yearly date with yourself from now on.

Packing for your 48-hour break
What to take:

- old clothes—you're not going out, except maybe to a local café
- career planning books you enjoy
- chocolate—a natural mood-lifter
- CDs of mood music
- one novel, to be read sparingly, late at night
- fresh roses to remind you of the importance of smelling them

What to ignore:

- the TV remote—this is about introspection not bad American sit-coms where everyone leads an 'amazing' life
- other people's expectations
- your past history—soooooo yesterday

Career segues

Are you a mover or a jumper?

Some of us are bold individuals who enjoy making radical changes, breathtaking leaps and, if we fall midstream, are prepared to cop the consequences. Think Richard Branson or Dick Smith or Gretel Killeen. Big personalities with big ideas who are prepared to take big risks. A demonstrably higher number of people like to make change slowly, to creep into a new space with no major fanfare, allowing themselves a chance to acclimatise. Neither way is the one 'right' way, and there are a lot of stages in between these two extremes.

When you understand the different ways of changing work, you are free to make change at a pace and in a way that does not feel frightening but, on the contrary, enthuses you to explore your own potential.

In *What Color is Your Parachute* Richard Bolles suggests there are two major moves you might make. You can change your role or you can change your industry type. There are other ways we can move, however. In Chapter 1 we considered the Connecting your career dots concept, which outlined six potential arenas of change.

- Sector
- Organisation
- Specific role
- Work arrangement
- Location
- Learning

Some of these changes are mutually exclusive, some are not. For instance, role enhancement can occur within the same company, or may involve moving to a different company in the same industry or to a different company in a different industry.

In Chapter 1 we met Trevor Barry and learnt how he took on the commitment of extra training in electrical work and refrigeration in order to gain qualifications which allowed him to range across a variety of tasks in the mines where he worked. These skills may not be directly related to his current role as an astronomer, but they certainly came in handy when he built his telescope. His current role required extra specific qualifications (his degree) and involved a change in three ways; role, company and industry. This was a radical change, but cushioned by a retrenchment package, completed gradually and fuelled by years of 'amateur' astronomy beforehand.

Let's revisit Table 1.1 where you began to Connect your career dots. If you haven't already done so, plot where you are right now, and whether it might be a role enhancement or change, and/ or a company/industry move that will allow you to enjoy a more meaningful working life. Or maybe you are ready for extra skills training or professional development. Use your 48-hour time out to revisit and fill in the moves you have made, and those you would like to make next.

Catherine Lockhart
The confidence factor

How can we review our experience and skills to find the things that matter?
Go back to where you've been and consider why you were good at what you did before. Talk about it, write it down. Define your transferable skills, and don't get caught up in the bigger job picture—often the smaller details tell us more. Australians are usually overly modest—you have to drag out of them what they are good at and help them break down their many skills. Young mums are often inclined to think they've lost the skills that they had in the workforce and forget to recognise those they've gained, such as multi-tasking. Often when mums go back to work they're amazed at what they can achieve, sometimes doing the same amount part time as they previously did full time.

How do we get started if we are scared of making a major change?
Ask yourself what is the worst thing that can happen if you make this change. This normally helps take the scare factor out. For many people the worst thing is that they don't try something new at all.

What if we feel hopelessly trapped by financial commitments, time constraints or family issues?
If a change to more meaningful work is impossible at this point then set some goals for later on. Try to work out what you can do now to set yourself up for the future. Don't get rid of you dreams altogether.

Maybe all you can do right now is to read a book about the subject of your dreams. Or perhaps volunteer. When I first wanted to do counselling I worked for LifeLine a few hours a week which gave me a feel for whether I could do this work in the future. I have a friend who took a day off work to spend it shadowing teachers at a local school as this was his hoped-for career path. He came away buoyed and excited—and it only cost him a day!

With whom can I share my plans?
Forget the nearest and dearest. You can't rely on someone with a vested interest in your life, but do need someone who is independent. This might mean a friend who is a good listener. This person must also be positive, not a naysayer, and if possible someone who has been there and done it in the same field, or a different one. It might mean more than one person. A visit to the professional coaches' website allows you to email a request for a coach and a description of the support you are seeking (see the Notes and Resources section). Up to ten coaches will respond with an outline of what they think they have to offer—pitches for your business, if you like.

Sometimes people are scared to share their dreams and think they don't 'deserve' to achieve them. I often think of the old saying, if you want to climb over the fence, first you must throw your hat over it. If you want to follow your dream, it starts with you saying it out loud.

Catherine Lockhart is a life coach, counsellor and owner of the website <www.busymothers.com.au>

Visualising your options

Don't you hate the word visualisation? I'm not sure why, but it seems to smack of some New Age stunt which guarantees to locate your 'authentic self' and most Australians just don't buy this slick, easy-sounding shortcut to Zen and the meaning of life. It's a difficult word to replace, however, when it's necessary to do some concentrated imagining of future possibilities. And while achieving an 'authentic self' might be a lifelong goal, imagining a better working life is a practical and crucial way to start your move. So let's get over the terminology and consider what might be involved in useful visualisation.

It's difficult to work toward something that is intangible. So it is with career planning; in order to explore your options, begin by focusing on a concrete example of one vocation.

Perhaps you have long harboured the desire to be a jewellery designer, but have settled for a career as a barista in the meantime. Unless you are able to really see yourself as a designer and understand the practical steps which will get you there, it's likely to remain a pipedream. There are many ways to research what a jewellery designer might do, and which qualifications will be helpful. In Chapter 5 we considered some of them. This is all part of necessary research, but let's start at the glamorous end and search on Google using the term 'jewellery designer'. On the day I did this I came up with at least four good (Australian) websites that inspired me to think of this as an exciting and fulfilling career.

Now it's over to you. Take an hour to canvass two possible future careers. Answer the following questions, applying them separately to the two different career options.

- What role will I fill?
- Which industry sector(s) has/have such roles?
- How many hours will I work each week?
- Will a micro, small or large business best suit this role?
- Will I own this business, be an employee or contract worker?
- What type of working environment will this role offer—or would I like to create?
- How many people will I typically deal with in a normal day?
- How much am I likely to be paid?

- How independent is this role likely to be? Will I report to someone else?
- Will I be communicating with peers/colleagues face-to-face or via the internet or telephone?
- Will I be a decision-maker all, some, or very little of the time?
- How formal will the working environment be? The back paddock, a local café or an office in a high-rise tower—or somewhere else?
- Will I be gaining new qualifications or learning new skills in this role both in the short term and long term?
- Will this role fit in with my family life?
- Will I be able to share or delegate the work to give me time to recharge my batteries when needed?
- How much fun will I have?

There is a lot of thinking involved in the above questions. The length of your answers will vary but the more fully you describe your ideal vocation, the more information you are processing and assessing. Try to think exclusively about one of your desired career options in one two-hour session, and to work on an alternative career in another two-hour planning period, separated by at least a day. This should ensure your responses and ideas are equally fresh for each option and that you give them the attention and passion they each deserve.

Decision time

'Did you ever have to make up your mind?' So sang The Lovin' Spoonful in 1966 when they portrayed the age-old teenage dilemma of two girls and one boy. Now it's *your* decision time and once again there is no one 'right' answer—just one that may suit you better than the other.

In reviewing your two competing career paths, try to consider the questions in Table 6.1, giving each alternative a mark out of ten according to how closely it answers the question.

Time to score

Add up the scores out of ten to achieve a potential score out of 80. Consider the career which has 'won' and then ask yourself the following questions:

• What are the things that worry me most about this role?
• Are they sufficient to stop me trying it?
• What (if any) substantial barriers are there to my entry in this field?
• Are they really enough to stop me?

Mulling it over

Now take a week off 'worrying' about this career change and just let your thoughts percolate so that by the end of seven days one of three things will have happened:

1. You will have a deepening sense of dread about going down this career path. It will feel all too risky and foolish and 'not you' and you will abandon the idea and start over on the search for meaningful work.

OR

2. You will feel largely unexcited by the idea of such a major change and decide you don't have the energy or enthusiasm to pursue it. You will decide that your current work is fine; with a little tweaking it could continue to interest, so you'll pass on the idea of change.

OR

3. You will experience increasing excitement at the thought that it just *might* be possible that you can do this work, and that it will indeed make your heart sing. It won't even feel like work, you will be very good at it and have a lot of fun. It will have become the 'itch' that won't go away.

Table 6.1 Competing career paths

	Option One	Option Two
Name of option		
Is this a good move for my current experience, skills and qualifications? Give a mark out of 10.		
What are the five things I would like most about this role (list five below and give them an importance ranking out of 10)		
	1. /10	1. /10
	2. /10	2. /10
	3. /10	3. /10
	4. /10	4. /10
	5. /10	5. /10
Is this a role I have considered for a long time?		
Is this a role others have noted I might be good at?		

Jen Bird:
A new Broome

I studied information management at university and graduated with a Bachelor of Social Science. My first job was with Mars Confectionary in trade marketing before I moved to Intrepid Travel. I started there as a tour leader, working in Indonesia for five years and I finished as the Global Public Relations Manager, based in Melbourne. It was a great job but a difficult one to develop. Initially the company didn't invest a lot of energy in PR and I had to fight hard to prove its importance and to make it a strong facet of the marketing program.

About four years ago my husband, James, who was working in finance, and I decided we wanted to live and work somewhere warm. We registered with an online business sale registry. We looked at a fish and chips shop, and a gardening business, and took four weeks' leave to travel the east coast to look at different locations and options. We needed to do that; to get away and have a serious look at what was out there.

In 2006 a business based in Broome, Kimberley Wild Expeditions, came up for sale. I'd been to Broome before but for James this move was a complete act of faith. He flew there to have a look at the business and let's just say his first night in Broome was a total shock to the system. But my experience in tourism was a real bonus, combined with his background in financial consulting and his ability to understand a balance sheet. I'd failed accounting three times; I just wasn't interested in that side.

So three years later, here we are. I look after the sales and marketing side as well as the tour preparation. The transferable skills I've brought across are my people skills—I just love working with people—my organisational ability and the fact that I work well under pressure. In fact, I thrive. One week after relocating I learnt I was pregnant with our daughter, so I certainly needed that ability to rise to the occasion. We've doubled the business in the past twelve months. We weren't really prepared to be this busy, so it would have been good to be more organised.

We love it here and consider the Kimberley to be Australia's last pristine wilderness. I'm Vice-President of Broome Visitor Centre. It's been a good way to meet other operators and get on top of what's happening. Having a new baby so soon after arriving meant we weren't able to be as social as we would have liked.

This move to such a remote town has been the best thing we've ever done, full of challenges. My advice to others contemplating such a change is to just do it!

If it doesn't work out, it's not the end of the world. We'll still have our shirts on our backs and our children. If you contemplate something for too long, the opportunity will probably pass by. And once it's gone, it's gone.

Jen Bird is co-owner of Kimberley Wild Expeditions
<www.kimberleywild.com.au>

Goals and deadlines

Most of us have been around long enough to have been exposed to the importance of setting goals. One of my least favourite clichés is that those who fail to plan, plan to fail. I've always found this just a touch glib—as well as untrue. We're not really planning to fail—we just don't like the formalised processes of goal- and deadline-setting— it seems much more natural, romantic even, to let things happen at their own pace.

Well, the sad truth is that this organic pace may be what you've settled for while your current career has stalled, and to make any forward movement you are actually going to need some measurable goals.

It's no coincidence that a goal is both the term which is used for scoring successfully in sport and for ambitions in our business and personal lives. When a team member scores a goal in a competitive game, hearts race and fists pump. Now this is *exactly* the type of feeling you should hope to achieve when you plan *your* goals.

Get it? Goal-setting is not a chore, but a series of small wins which add up to a large score. Think of these wins as a means to an end. It is all about creating a clear, definable, measurable work outcome which will thrill you. Until you have such a goal you are likely to waste time on things that won't advance your cause and maybe miss opportunities which could greatly enhance your chances of finding the work you want.

So how do you set your goals as painlessly as possible?

Start by listing, in Table 6.2, three main things you wish to achieve; one short term, one medium and one long term. An example is provided to get your thinking started.

Getting smarter

You've probably heard about SMART goals before now. This acronym refers to goals which are Specific, Measurable, Achievable, Realistic, and to a Timeline. These are the goals that you stand a chance of achieving because they are attainable—not some pie-in-the-sky dream which is tantalising, but ultimately frustrating. The key point about SMART goals is that if your goals fit these criteria you are much more likely to reach them. It may be stating the obvious, but it's a point we often miss when we daydream about running a cutting-edge consultancy business but refuse to qualify and quantify how this will fit into our rather messy lives.

So let's look at the setting of deadlines, and see how they might fit into your goal-setting plan.

Your first move

You've already divided your plans into short, medium and long term. Review your short-term goal and decide on an action which will ensure this will be achievable within the day. It might be a phone call, visiting a website, the local library; something you can actually

Table 6.2 Goal-setting

Goal	Short term	Medium term	Long term
Example	Take Mum to war photograph exhibition at local gallery and ask her to tell me about her time in Korea	Write 1500 word article about my mother's experiences during the Korean War	Move from my current role as library assistant to full-time author in two years, being able to live off my income from writing
Completion Date	**Within 14 days**	**Within 30 days**	**Within two years**
Starting Points	*Today* Phone Mum and confirm she is available	*Within a week* Do preliminary research about Mum's service records on National Archives website	*Within a month* Research writing courses in my state
Your goals	**Short term**	**Medium term**	**Long-term**
Completion date	**Within 14 days**	**Within 30 days**	**Within 2 years**
Starting Points	*Today*	*Within a week*	*Within a month*

do today so you can go to bed tonight knowing you have made a start. If it is a phone call, perhaps to make a time to talk to someone about your new career goals, this is a HUGE start. Because once you start the ball rolling, it will gather momentum in spite of you! People will call you back, take the time to share their knowledge and maybe introduce you to other people who can also help. So when you feel overwhelmed and discouraged, you will have already generated enough activity to carry the whole project forward. If I am making this sound simple, it's because it is. It is the direct result of taking action and building momentum.

Now consider a second round of quick actions to move all your goals forward. List them all, with deadlines similar to the first round and note how much closer you are to achieving all your goals. When it all boils down, if you follow the plan the motivation will take care of itself. Ask any successful sales person and they will tell you that the number of calls they make is directly proportionate to their ultimate sales achievements. The more calls they make, the more they sell. Simple as that.

Staying put

You took the 48-hour break and feel refreshed and happy to go back to work.

Lucky you. Not everyone wants to throw in a perfectly good job and take a chance on the unknown. Why would they when they have worked for a long time to earn their place in an organisation or created a viable business? If this is your situation it doesn't necessarily mean that you don't want a change. It might mean that you would like to reinvent your current role, tweaking it to better suit who you are now, compared with the person you were five, ten or twenty years ago.

And as the need for skilled workers increases, your chances of successfully renegotiating your current role just get better. Are there risks associated with this? Most definitely. But, properly researched and managed, the potential rewards are greater.

First, you will need to ascertain those aspects of the job you wish to keep—and those you would happily lose. There's no point in throwing out the baby with the bathwater. Consider your current role. List the five things you really enjoy doing, and five you would rather delegate to someone else. Consider also the wider aspects of this role—the company, the remuneration, your working hours, work environment, colleagues and travel time. Which make you want to stay and which are less appealing?

Now think about your value to this company. Are you up to speed on where your company is heading? Just as your employer may not realise you have grown and developed in new ways over the past few months or years, so you, too, may be out of touch with your company's new directions and achievements. Most organisations, whether not-for-profits, multinationals or the local car wash, have an internet presence. Visit your company's website and read the mission statement, the 'about' page and the annual report—whichever brings you up-to-date most quickly.

Your pitch

Now you are in a better position to understand how your skills and talents might continue to add value to your employer. Write a list of your achievements that relate to this current role and employer and add some thoughts about potential future projects in which you would like to be involved. You may have added value as an 'operative' in the past, but maybe there exists a useful role as a teacher, trainer, mentor or someone who can document valuable IP (intellectual property) in the future.

Bear in mind how expensive it is for companies to replace staff. If replacing you means your company may need to employ the services of a headhunter, for instance, this can cost a few or many thousands of dollars, depending upon your seniority and salary. There are also the 'on costs' to factor in—each replacement employee will need training and a familiarisation period, so it is in the interests of your current boss to keep you on purely for financial reasons, let alone your intrinsic worth to the company. Remembering this—perhaps even pointing it out—also translates into a confidence booster at the time of renegotiation of your work role.

Getting what you want

You now have a list of achievements—past and some possible future projects—and can start to offer some thoughts on changing your role to include more work which will challenge and reward you—and prove of great value to your employer. Now turn your list into a proposal. List all the new work you would like to do, and, if appropriate, any courses or training you will be willing to undertake to help expand your role. Now consider the trade-offs you are prepared to make. And don't fool yourself that this is a one-way conversation where you will walk into your boss's office and get exactly what you want. That is highly unlikely. The best strategy is to work out in advance what you are prepared to give that will help your organisation to offer you a better job. Some of the following trade-offs may work for you:

- Downsizing your week. Maybe you work a 40-hour week. Suggest you work four days at nine hours, and the other four hours can be taken as leave owing. This reduces the company's financial obligations and suddenly gives you a magic extra day—enough to enthuse anyone!
- Offer to telecommute one or more days per week. Again, this can be a win-win—you have a pyjama day, get rid of non-paid commuting time, maybe even enjoy a leisurely breakfast with your nearest and dearest and your company gets the same work—or perhaps an even more productive input.
- Offer to start training other staff and sharing your long-term intellectual property—maybe even suggest your involvement in documenting systems and processes and a company manual. These are often areas which companies are going to 'get around to', but never do. To be offered an in-house chronicler might be

a blessed relief to a harried middle manager who is aware of the company's vulnerability in this area.

- Ask for time off on a regular basis to work as a volunteer—or extended leave, maybe on half-pay to commit to a volunteer program. You may find this reignites your enthusiasm for your day job without any other changes. Maybe another colleague would like to do the same thing? Maybe your company is prepared to commit to a needy cause on an ongoing basis and you can offer to manage this commitment, thus adding meaning to your day job without the need to leave!

Selling it

Okay, enough with the ideas—you get the drift. Now add some of your own thoughts and formalise your proposal in a way that is both interesting and enticing to an employer who wants you to stay, but needs to be convinced you can modify your role and still add value.

Next, decide which person you should approach. In a larger organisation it may be expected that you will go through the Human Resources (HR) department. But if you feel the HR manager is too inexperienced or unsympathetic to understand this renegotiation, don't shoot yourself in the foot. Choose the colleague you consider the most senior and intuitive and run it past him or her—asking if they are prepared to be a (discreet) sounding board. If they feel this proposal has merit they may even endorse it as it goes through the 'proper channels'. Next, book the significant other, the teenage son, a trusted friend, even the family dog, and role-play your negotiation. Yes, it may sound corny, but more practice means a smoother delivery and in turn a much higher likelihood of succeeding. You're almost ready.

Spend the day before the renegotiation making sure your grooming is as good as it gets. Now you're ready—you're giving this your best shot, and you're sure to be persuasive because you've done the research, thought it through and are offering some tangible benefits to your employer. If you get a knockback, don't let it worry you too

Table 6.3 Removing obstacles		
Possible obstacles	**Your List**	**Possible remedies or ways or reducing importance of this obstacle**
Insufficient skills		
Insufficient experience		
Lack of education		
Lack of qualifications		
Lack of self-confidence		
Lack of relevant contacts		
Financial constraints		
Other		

much. You've already done the hard yards for a career segue towards some other, more worthy, employer.

Tackling roadblocks

One of the surefire ways of not achieving what you hope for is to ignore the things that *might* go wrong and then feel disappointed or become derailed if they do. Optimism is a great quality, but not anticipating potential problems only means you are totally unprepared for them when they come your way, as they often do.

So before you launch into your next career move, or book an appointment with the boss to discuss a change in your current role, why not take the time to consider obstacles that may occur—and what you will do if they turn up?

Some of the most common reasons you will not get the role or career you are seeking is a perceived shortfall in your work DNA—your skills, your experience, your achievements, your qualifications. There may also be more personal reasons, such as your self-confidence, or your health. Some of these perceived shortcomings may not be able to be solved quickly. And that isn't the point. The skill lies in knowing what you can do to minimise these problems rather than totally annihilate them. Wound the dragon so his tail doesn't move rather than cut it off entirely.

Which weak spots impair your ability to make the career move that appeals? Fill in Table 6.3 against any categories where you consider you have a weak spot. Then consider the third column which asks you to come up with a partial remedy.

One more thing. Sheer optimism won't get you through, but a little positive thinking can take you a long way!

The human touch

This chapter has been particularly heavy on introspection. That's because it's important to focus on what you want without being overly influenced by other people's agendas. Hopefully by now you have managed to do that and have a useful plan with an achievable long-term goal, and some short- and medium-term 'to dos' along the way. If so, now might be the perfect time to consult an honest friend.

We saw in Chapter 4 how effectively Peter Hatherley is using his 'mirror' mentor in the pursuit of his acting career. While we all like to claim a wide friendship group, the reality is there are probably just one or two friends who will stand up and be counted. This is the sort of friend who loves you enough to tell you the truth—even when you don't want to hear it. It's great to plan to do big things, but often it's even better to introduce a reality check before we head into the wide world, lights flashing. So if you have someone (not family) who is prepared to listen, evaluate, and respond with constructive feedback, now is the time to share your dream. If, after listening to your plans, they reel back in horror, this doesn't necessarily mean you are on the wrong track—but it could be an indication that some fine-tuning is necessary, or that there are other potential obstacles which you have missed and these need addressing before you invest your superannuation in the market garden built on a toxic rubbish dump!

And why, pray, should you not share this dream with the family? That's entirely up to you, but sometimes our family members have a strong vested interest in our staying exactly where we are. Maybe your ageing mum will be just too lonely if you move to Colombia to teach English for a year? Maybe your father is thinking of the thousands upon thousands of dollars he invested in your law degree and the idea of you trying out as a standup comedian in the corner pub is a little too alarming? Maybe your wife really does want to have that fourth child—the long-desired daughter after three sons—and the prospect of increasing the mortgage to pay living costs while you train as a landscape gardener is too big a leap for her imagination?

Whatever the scenario is—I think you get my drift.

Chapter wrap

There is one recurring message in this chapter. We've looked at the basics of planning and recognised the importance of a 48-hour break to consider two different future work possibilities. Next we have worked through a series of concrete actions to help you appraise these options and to set some goals to bring this change about. We've also considered the very real possibility that it may not be necessary for you to change your current role/employer, just to renegotiate the conditions of the work, refining it into something more fulfilling and enjoyable. Once your goal has been clarified and a future path chosen, the continuing thread is in the need to qualify and quantify the way you will achieve what you want. If 'a series of small steps' was good enough for Van Gogh to achieve his works of art and a 'first step' was enough to get Chairman Mao started on the Long March, then it should certainly get the rest of us closer to full enjoyment of our talents.

Connecting the career dots

Ella James is irrepressible—thirteen sackings and she's still kicking goals. At the time of writing she had just performed at the 2009 Helpmann Awards at the Sydney Opera House. Her current work requires similar skills to those in her previous gigs as a radio announcer but without the 'security' of a pay cheque. Instead she contracts for work projects, both teaches and attends classes as a student, and puts herself 'out there' on open-mike nights at comedy festivals.

Jen Bird has remained in the travel sector, using her transferable skills to build and promote the Kimberley Wild Expeditions tour operating business. Her hard-won lessons in PR and marketing are more than relevant to her current role. She and her husband have enjoyed their move from city to the outback as well as the challenges of running their own show. As a newcomer, her role as Vice-President of the Broome Visitor Centre offers strong local networking opportunities and activities.

7

Selling your talents

Many of us were raised by the old adage that 'self-praise is no recommendation'. When it comes to securing work, however, following this motto is guaranteed to have a crippling effect on your performance in an interview or work pitch. But how do you strike that fine line between successfully representing your skills, attributes and experience—and boasting? This chapter looks at how people get hired—and it's little surprise that word-of-mouth or personal connections are trumps. If you're not currently well connected in the field of your dreams, you'll need to do some research, meet the right people and use this information to good effect to assist you to land the crucial meeting or interview. Viewing interview opportunities as a 'meeting of equals' and conducting yourself both professionally and with confidence are also important strategies. There is no one right way to sell your talents but many effective strategies you can adopt to further your cause.

From fantasy to reality

Dreaming about meaningful work, researching industries and roles and meeting people who can inspire your progress are important precursors to applying for a new role. They can also be very enjoyable activities. But sooner or later the research has to stop and the application and interviewing process must begin. Whether we are applying for paid employment or a contractual or consultancy role, after we have done our research the next step is to prepare a sales pitch which not only accurately reflects our suitability for the desired project, but also the degree of experience, energy and professionalism which will win us the work. It's not a pipedream, but an entirely achievable proposition.

Alan Maxwell:
Trikeman

I've been in Information Technology (IT) for more than 21 years, originally with the public service but for the past six years as a consultant. I wish I'd started contracting ten or fifteen years ago. I don't feel insecure as a consultant as I try to do good work, and the rates are lucrative. My projects run for a short period so if I'm not happy I can easily move on. I once worked in a really hostile work environment and made up my mind if it ever happened again I would get straight out of there.

It's a lot of fun, it's not difficult or physically demanding and we're both hoping it will become our retirement income.

Three years ago my wife and I moved from our house on the Mornington Peninsula to a flat in Melbourne's Docklands precinct. Both our jobs meant leaving home at 6.30 am and travelling for hours, not getting back until 7 or 8 pm. Taking a flat in the city has saved us about fifteen hours of commuting a week. With the kids through school and university, and some disposable income, I decided to go out and buy a Harley. But I test-drove a Chopper 4, made by Australian company OZ Trikes, and I was hooked. The trike can accommodate a rider and up to three passengers so I gave some people a lift and they just loved it. I wondered if I could turn it into a business and so Tours on Trike was born. My wife, Joh, and I had run a computer repair business previously but that had been fairly stressful. The continuing need to hit the mortgage for funding felt like putting your balls on the line, time and again, just to let someone hit them with a bat. I hated being beholden to a bank manager who can make you a winner or a loser with a stroke of the pen.

This business is different. For a start it's a lot of fun, it's not difficult or physically demanding and we're both hoping it will become our retirement income. To start up we needed a driver's accreditation certificate, which is not quite as onerous as a taxi driving licence, as well as a police, licence and medical check and public liability insurance. My IT background has been handy when establishing our website. We've also put a lot of energy into creating promotional material and getting the message out there. We've invested fairly heavily in Tours on Trike over the past twelve months but it's starting to pay back and it should be self-funding this year.

Not a ride goes by that a taxi driver doesn't pull down his window and say, 'Hey mate, do you want to swap?'

And I don't. I'm having too much fun where I am.

Alan Maxwell is the co-owner of Tours on Trike and an IT consultant <www.toursontrike.com.au>

A tailored approach

What is the best approach to selling *your* talents?

Many theories abound and many 'experts' are so adamant that it's their way or the highway that it can seem that much of the information on this tricky subject serves only to confuse rather than illuminate. It shouldn't have to be this hard.

The three very different ways of seeking work can be summarised as follows:

1. It's basically a numbers game: the more work you apply for, the more quickly you will succeed.
2. It's anything *but* a numbers game. You must work smart, not hard and cut back on the number of interviews you seek.
3. Not going after a new job, but just taking it as it comes, is the best way to define your new career self.

The first approach seems to advocate frenetic activity in a short period of time (the gung-ho method). The second suggests a more cerebral and refined approach, let's call it 'less is more'. And the third advocates a rather stately drift towards something more thrilling. Let's call this one the 'organic' method.

Whilst very different, these three methods are each based on sensible rationales, so it shouldn't be necessary to treat them as mutually exclusive. It's useful to examine them more closely in order to adopt the best aspects for your particular situation and dump the rest.

But first, let's consider the maths behind the selection process. How do companies find people to do the work required? Has it indeed 'all gone online' or does there remain a glimmer of hope for those of us troglodytes who like to speak and meet with real people when future work is at stake?

How are people hired?

There are many different ways organisations and prospective employees or workers find each other. The following eight in Table 7.1 are the most common.

The figure in the right-hand column is the stated success rate of this approach as defined by Mark Emery Bolles and Richard Nelson Bolles in *Job Hunting Online*. These statistics refer to the American market only. They still, however, provide a useful indication with

Table 7.1 Finding work	
Method	**Likely success rate**
Answering newspaper advertisements	Depending upon salary levels, 5% (higher salaries)—24% (lower salaries)
Visiting a government employment office	14%
Private employment agency (temp agencies excluded)	5%
Sending résumés to random employers	7%
Posting résumé on online career site	4% (up to 10% in IT)
Asking friends and acquaintances	33%
Cold calls to business premises	47%
Contacting companies after researching their relevance to your career goals	69%

Complied from conclusions in Bolles & Bolles *Job Hunting Online*

which to judge the potential of finding a new job if you just post your résumé online and hope like hell someone out there finds you.

The good news is that, since your application is so unlikely to be located and selected for an interview via the online process, the old-fashioned personal skills you have honed over the years are just as likely to stand you in good stead in your job search. The bad news is that, if you believe the Bolles' numbers, you will need to stick your head up above the parapet and do some cold calling to get what may be a successful interview. When seeking work you will need to take a risk, and then another, and then another still.

So whilst it is difficult to gauge real numbers for different job search methods in Australia, you will need energy, application and ingenuity if you wish to stand out from the pack. Armed with this information, let's reconsider the three different approaches to finding a new job and consider which aspects might work best for you.

The gung-ho approach

This is the method most commonly associated with the previously cited Richard Bolles in his exceptionally successful job-hunting 'bible' *What*

Color is Your Parachute? For those wishing to reconsider their career directions and ways in which they might make a positive change, this is a terrific book full of helpful ideas and insights. It does, however, tend to over-emphasise the 'get out there and pound the pavement 24/7' approach, sometimes at the expense of a more considered strategy.

'You must spend 35 hours a week, at least, on your search for one of the jobs that are out there. That should cut down, dramatically the number of weeks it takes you to find work—moreso, than any other factor,' says Richard Bolles.

Does this seem like a quantity over quality approach? The more applications you make, the sooner you will be successful in landing one of these jobs? Perhaps. But where Bolles is at his best is when he encourages persistence. And this quality of persistence might be even more effective when applied to the next way of approaching your role change.

Less is more

This approach is very well explained (if a little repetitively) in *Ask the Headhunter,* written by (you guessed it) a headhunter named Nick Corcodilos. Corcodilos maintains that the truly successful job hunter or work seeker will eschew most interviews on the grounds that there are few jobs out there which really suit their particular suite of talents. Instead he urges those seeking a new position to refine the actual role for which they are prepared to apply in order to avoid catching 'interviewitis', a condition which afflicts those who front up for a lot of positions, but are rarely hired. This approach fits much more neatly with management expert David Maister's advice 'Forget what's available out there. Go after the job you really want the most.'

Corcodilos believes that the critical strategy for successful job change is to focus on just four key questions, and test their match to the position advertised:

1. Do you understand the job that needs to be done?
2. Can you do the job?

3. Can you do the job the way the employer/hirer wants it done?
4. Can you do the job profitably for the company?

It is Corcodilos' contention that, if you can truthfully answer these four questions, you will effectively reduce the number of jobs for which you will apply, while dramatically increasing your chances of winning those you really want and believe you can do well.

There seems to be a lot of sense in this approach, mainly because it forces those seeking a new role or a new placement to do their homework *before* they risk their self-esteem on being knocked back for something that probably wouldn't suit them anyway. This approach also saves valuable time, allowing job changers to focus more on what matters most—the work they would really like to be doing.

The 'organic' approach

This way of tackling career change is outlined in *Working Identity* by Herminia Ibarra, Professor of Organisational Behavior at INSEAD in France. Ibarra maintains that too much reflection and introspection on career moves is counterproductive and that we need to act first. This action will then lead to knowledge which will build our courage and networks leading us towards a new future, even if we have no idea, at the outset, what that future might be. Ibarra supports a wonderfully 'Zen' form of surrender to the universe, mixed somewhat conversely with a strong dose of American zeal for the power of networks. Whilst *Working Identity* tends to focus on stories of those in senior positions in large organisations (thus potentially alienating a huge swathe of the working population), it does have a refreshing message—*don't say it, do it*. Or, as Ella James, profiled in Chapter 6, insists, 'If you want your life to change, you need to change your life.'

Using your judgment

So what wisdom can we extract from these very different strategies?

The first, obvious, lesson is that one size does not fit all and at certain times in our lives one of these approaches might be more effective than another. Consider the recently retrenched social worker who is used to working 50 hours a week. Replacing the social contacts, structure and 'busyness' of her previous occupation may be important so that she doesn't feel as though she has fallen into a bottomless void. So adopting the 35-hour per week 'your job is to get a job' gung-ho approach might help this activity-deprived person feel as though she is doing something to further her cause. The opposite argument, of course, is that it might do her good to kick back and reflect before hurling herself into a similarly busy, and perhaps no more satisfying, role, just so she can tick the box that she got another job, with added brownie points for doing so really quickly.

These are the kind of judgments only you can make, depending upon a number of personal factors. As long as you are entirely honest about these factors, and not just trying to fool yourself because you are scared of sticking your neck out, you will probably choose the right course.

Combined wisdom

The approaches may vary but one point on which all the above-mentioned authors are consistent is the necessity to know well the area in which you hope to excel. You need to do the research and become an expert in the areas which interest you the most. Whether you do this research on the internet, face-to-face, by phone, or by other methods is where the authors vary, but all are consistent on the fact that there is no substitute for knowing your greener pastures.

Chapters 3 and 4 encouraged you to dig deep to understand the type of work which will best suit your skills, experience and aptitudes. Chapter 6 helped you narrow your thinking to two possible career moves. Now it's time to do some specific research on each of these alternatives to see which one stands the test of scrutiny. This research can be tackled by considering the broader work context of these roles and by conducting at least five informational interviews. In other words, by combining the theory with some face-to-face knowledge acquisition.

Seeking context

We often hear the phrase that we should learn to see things in context. There's a good reason why, when it comes to a new career path or role. It comes back to the old adage of not seeing the wood for the trees; in this case the opportunity for the 'known knowns'. Former US Secretary of State, Donald Rumsfeld, was much maligned a few years back when he got himself into a tortuous verbal dead-end by discussing 'known knowns' and 'known unknowns'. In fact, he's still up on YouTube for those who like watching linguistic train wrecks. But 'known knowns' can be a very useful phrase when it comes to considering what you might miss unless you re-evaluate the context of your preferred work.

Events coordinator

Consider your possible desire to become an events coordinator. You currently work as a personal assistant to a manager in an IT company. You know little about event management, just what you've seen by visiting the occasional exhibition, as well as what your friend, Brad, told you at a party a few weeks ago.

You need to know a lot more before pursuing this career.

To give some context to this vocation, first do a search on the previously mentioned *Job Guide* website (details are listed in the Notes and Resources section) which offers a realistic job description and a list of institutions in your state that offer training and dates when the next courses start.

Armed with this information on the specific role, next you will need to ascertain where this occupation fits in the grand scheme of things and what you might typically earn. To do this, visit the DEEWR Australian Jobs website, also previously mentioned. Here you can check out the economic sector, the industry and many further details on the future prospects for this type of work. There's little point in setting your heart on becoming an organ grinder's monkey if there's just one position going and a monkey named Pierre has beaten you to it!

Start with the industry profiles and take a stab at the correct industry terminology. For events coordinator, maybe property and business services sound as though they fit. The first thing to note is the percentage employment change over the past five years. In this instance it's showing a growth of 17 per cent—healthy! Further reading reveals that this is Australia's second largest employing industry, with strong prospects. In fact employment growth is predicted to remain strong over the coming five years with 157,000 new jobs anticipated. Most other indicators are in line with all industries (percentage of older workers, females, part-time positions available) with the exception of employment outside capital cities; it is only 27 per cent rather than the Australian average of 37 per cent. Two other websites also offer useful background for those interested in such a career path: <http://degreedirectory.org/articles/Event_Coordinator_Career_Definition_Job_Outlook_and_Training_Requirements.html> and <http://www.ehow.com/facts_5022830_event-coordinator-planning-careers.html>.

Now look up the job prospects matrix for detail such as gender ratio, unemployment likelihood, median age of workers, likely earnings and future jobs growth. Even those who are not currently seeking a change of job will find the statistics fascinating as they tell the story of the move to quaternary and quinary jobs as noted by futurist Phil Ruthven in Chapter 5, but fleshed out with the names of real jobs that are coming—and those that are disappearing.

Those who still don't feel they have enough context for the type of occupation they think they might enjoy, can try further mining the education and training links in the *Job Guide* for even more information.

Enough with the statistics—it's time to warm up your search with some people contact.

The informational interview

People need to take a much more creative approach to delivering value in the emerging marketplace—this is very different from 'finding a job'. The formal 'job' market—reached through advertised roles and recruiters, represents only a small percentage of the real work opportunities out there. The wider marketplace for work can only be discovered by running lots of conversations with as wide a range of people as possible, exploring what is happening in their organisations, opening doors, developing ideas with them. Networking—which is what we are talking about here, is not 'selling yourself', it is about discovery, about research-driven conversations founded on well-thought-through questions and an active interest in other people and the organisations they work in. Most of us can do with a little coaching here.

—Hugh Davies, Macfarlan Lane

Plenty of authors and career experts have written at length on the subject of the informational interview, often in such a theoretical way it becomes a real turn-off to anyone considering undertaking one. I don't plan to add to the deluge, except to recount a personal story.

My first experience of the informational interview occurred when I was a 19-year-old third-year student at Emily McPherson College in Melbourne, studying for a Diploma in Fashion Design and Production. Our communication teacher, Miss Breen, was determined that all of her design students would be employed. She requested that we apply for and undergo at least three informational interviews before we applied for a 'real' job. Her reasoning was that exposure to people who knew a lot about the type of job we might want would build our knowledge, our networks and supply much-needed interview experience. She also warned us that we were there for the information only; we must not expect the interviewer to offer us a job. It wasn't the point of the exercise and wouldn't happen. And we must follow up with a thank-you note.

I was one of the few, to my knowledge, to take on board Miss Breen's suggestion. And the funny thing is, more than 30 years later, I still remember meeting those captains of the fashion industry, and their willingness to spend the time helping a student learn more about how their industry ticked. Miss Breen was right about how generous successful people tend to be, but wrong about the job part. Subsequently all of them offered me a job! Valuable contacts indeed!

Questions to ask

How do you structure an informational interview?

The aim of this meeting is to make the discussion as efficient and productive as possible. You are trying to gain a fuller understanding of the type of work which is done in certain roles, in certain industries. You are looking for insider knowledge that can be added to the information you already have to help you form a picture of how *you* might add value to this industry in a similar or complementary role. It could also help you understand that this role/industry is vastly different from what you thought and the idea of such work is very unappealing.

Useful questions are:

1. Do you like your current role?
2. What are the really standout aspects of it?
3. Which parts are less appealing?
4. Is this a good industry to be in? Why or why not?
5. Are there associated roles or industries worth exploring?
6. Where is your career path headed? What fresh challenges do you see for yourself, your company, your sector?
7. How do you stay abreast of new developments in your industry?
8. Do you have a personal development regime?
9. Who do you admire most in your industry? Do you know them? Is it possible for me to use your name if I approach them for a similar chat?
10. What type of roles did you have which led to this one? Which were helpful? Which less so?
11. Were any particular educational qualifications necessary? Is this still the case?

12. If you were looking for someone to replace yourself, which qualities would be mandatory, and which negotiable?

13. Are there any new roles starting to emerge in this industry? Can you describe how they vary from previous positions?

14. If you were in my shoes, what would you do to learn more about this type of work?

15. Are there any particular associations that you consider important to join?

16. Is there a body of information, or ongoing media, that you would recommend?

Shut up and listen

These questions are, by their very nature, broad and therefore applicable to a wide range of roles from tour guide to clock-maker to business angel. Brief answers to all of them should be possible within a 50-minute interview, as long as you listen, take useful notes and don't interject. It is possible that your discussion will lead your subject to ask a lot about you and your plans—this is not the purpose of your interview, but may be an indication that they feel you have sufficient value to recommend to a colleague or acquaintance, or to bear in mind for future projects. All well and good. It's also worth noting that the priority of the above questions is on the *now*, on staying current and valuable and informed in a work sense. It's not about the traditional interview style of where did it all start—school, education, first job, leading to the where are you now?, where are you headed? questions. History is a wonderful tool for learning not to make the same mistakes too many times over. But in a rapidly changing world of work, it is important to stop looking into a rearview mirror and to start looking ahead, far ahead, before someone else overtakes you.

Living with the natives

This is a term used by the 'headhunter' Nick Corcodilos who urges work seekers to: 'Try to spend your time with people who are happy and successful at the kind of work you want to do . . . You will learn things (including where to find such jobs) that are inaccessible to outsiders.'

Career counsellor Dr Peter Carey describes this practice as 'shadowing' successful people. Whatever the nomenclature, there are two main reasons for this approach. Firstly, you will learn more about your target work from those who do it than from any other source. Given that these practitioners are also successful, the odds are that their insight is best practice, their knowledge current and their attitude generous. Successful people usually have little problem in sharing their insights and, more often than not, enjoy helping others who have drive, energy and enthusiasm. The second reason for spending time in the company of those who are good at what they do, is because their companionship is positive and beneficial to you. You will not create the blueprint for a successful second, third or fourth career by mixing with those who are tired, frustrated or negative, or who delight in telling you what you cannot do. You will, however, gain top-quality inside information from knowledgeable natives.

Fiona Corr*:
Back to the books

Like most things in my life, my first career choice happened purely by accident. A teacher at my school thought she saw potential and so offered me free violin lessons. I moved to viola and despite my headmistress's expectations that I would pursue a high-powered law or medical career, I decided to follow music. She even 'cautioned' me about a life on stage but I think this just appealed to my rebellious teenage nature. Either way, I came out of Melbourne University with a Bachelor in Music and Education. The teaching skill was really in case I needed a fallback position. During my degree I had many wonderful opportunities to perform with the Victorian State

Opera and to peform in Tokyo, London, Paris and Vienna as well as to record in Australia.

But I discovered that it wasn't a sustainable lifestyle; I'd be at home practising during the day and playing at night. I'd met my husband-to-be, Eddie, and thought we could have a good long-term relationship if only we had some time together. Someone once told me you can't have a career, a partner and children. You can only ever expect to do two successfully; one has to give. I've certainly made a few less-than-ideal career choices to support the family. In the 1980s I had many happy years as head of music at two private schools. I managed to juggle the work with caring for our first child, taking just five months' maternity leave, but when the second came I took the hard decision not to return.

After this I went into some sort of mourning for my professional life, then I had a long, hard think and decided if I was a mum, I would give it my best shot, and became incredibly focused on my children. After a couple of years I did some part-time music teaching at a girls' school and had the opportunity to expand this role. But I knew I had to do something different. We were finally getting on our feet financially and I had a restless feeling, a sense that I was meant to do something more.

I considered my choices and realised being a full-time mother was not a satisfying long-term solution. To pursue a full-time music career was extremely demanding and given my commitments, I would only do this badly. So it was probably wise to find something different. And once I'd entertained that possibility it became a very exciting way to go!

Next I asked myself what skills I had, what I could actually do in a work sense. This made me feel vulnerable, but I looked back to my school days when I was good at pretty well anything. And the idea of re-skilling for me meant a return to university and I felt doubly excited at that prospect. I just love the learning process. I contacted VTAC (Victorian Tertiary Admissions Centre) and enquired how I would go as a mature-age student wishing to attempt a new degree. To my amazement my old HSC (Higher School Certificate) score was recorded and converted into the new measure, the ENTER score. And a very snappy one at that. To top it off, the lady on the phone told me, 'With this score you can do anything you like.'

I had a restless feeling, a sense that I was meant to do something more.

I was off and running.

I got the VTAC subject list—to me it was a telephone book of possibilities—and the psychology courses just jumped out at me, in particular a double major at Swinburne University which combines Psychology and Psychophysiology. It involves understanding brainwaves so I was hooked. As a teacher I had long wondered about the capacity of children to learn and here was a subject which would allow me to explore this more. I've achieved the first degree and am now working on a combined masters/PhD at Melbourne University.

Entry to this postgraduate degree was based on academic performance and an interview with a panel of three supervisors. I found this very confronting. I'd only ever experienced an interview for my first job. After this I'd been in the happy situation of being headhunted. They asked some ridiculous questions, including, 'Can you tell us about your weaknesses?'

I was confident because of my marks, but I needed to think quickly to answer this one. My reply was that I have many weaknesses, but that I believe maturity gives you strength and the capability to deal with your weaknesses and not let them get in the way.

I'm in the course, so I can only assume it was the right reply.

Fiona Corr* (not her real name) is a mature-age Masters/PhD student

Effective networking

If there is one thing guaranteed to make a roomful of Australians go silent it's the suggestion that they need to start networking. It is amazing how culturally different we are in this regard from Americans, who seem to place far higher store on the importance and benefits of networking. Most Australians seem to associate the business of networking with the activity of 'working' a roomful of strangers, pressing upon them a never-ending flow of business cards and talking about yourself. Truly productive networking involves the exact opposite. Careers adviser Hugh Davies sees it as taking a keen interest in a range of people with different lives and careers. So whilst you may 'live with the natives' to learn more about a career target, you may learn more in a general sense from people with very different backgrounds.

The major skill a networker needs to learn is to shut their mouth and open their ears. As the parent said to the teenager, 'It's not about *you*.' Well, networking is not really about *you*, either. It's about the wider world, how other people manage their careers, negotiating their way forwards, falling backwards, zigzagging sideways and coping with adversity as it occurs. What's fun? What works? What doesn't? Who do you know who is really good at this? It may well be that cards are exchanged—but hopefully because the person you have met wants to keep in touch, or maybe you've referred to something that interests them and you've promised to send them a copy or a weblink on this subject? When you learn to stop thinking of networking as card sharing and think of it as learning by listening you'll know you've nailed it.

Discriminating research

Data is not knowledge and knowledge is not wisdom, we are told. This becomes even more evident when we consider what might be important to know to stay abreast of vocational information. There is no end to what we might access and absorb. But with a limited number of hours in the day, it is evermore important to assess the value of our sources of information and focus on those that add most to our quest to find and do satisfying work.

Depending upon the field in which you wish to work, it is likely that you will be able to find information in daily papers, trade journals or magazines, on television, radio, or the internet. If you are already working full time, there is only so much information you will be able to handle, so consider reading the business section of one daily newspaper, subscribing to one specialist magazine or trade journal (go to the local library, check all possible journals for your preferred role/industry, and pick the most accessible and authoritative), and checking radio and TV guides in case there are programs which highlight aspects of the work you are keen to do. Using the internet is akin to opening Pandora's box, but maybe there are two or three great sites which are relevant to your career interests, as well as one or two general ones such as the Smart Company website or that of the *Harvard Business Review*. (Details are listed in the Notes and Resources section.) Beware of what appear to be informative business sites that require you to pay for content. No matter how good the site is, odds are this information will be available for free elsewhere. It really shouldn't be necessary to use your credit card to access quality information.

Securing a position

Here are two main options:

- *Option 1:* wait until your newly researched 'dream' ad pops up online or in a newspaper and both you and 4,500 other potential applicants see it. Then respond with a résumé and a request for an interview.
- *Option 2:* create your own position description—and matching résumé—and approach a handful of carefully selected companies for whom you would crawl over hot coals to work.

In the case of the first option, the numbers, as we have seen, are well and truly stacked against you finding satisfying work, with only 20 per cent of people being hired using methods in the visible market, namely recruitment firms and online or classified advertising. There is a case, of course, for adopting both methods. This might increase your chances as long as the only interviews you accept are those where you are convinced you like the work, can fill the role effectively, and are genuinely excited at the thought of working for the employer.

Robust résumés

For most people, creating a professional and engaging résumé is something akin to being asked to swallow castor oil. We know it will be good for us, but it's about the last thing we want to do. This might be due to a basic reluctance to be seen to talk up our own achievements. It may be that the tedious detail of qualifications or experiences from years, sometimes decades, ago have slipped our minds and it's all too hard to drag this detail out again—something similar to doing a tax return with a lurking suspicion we will get it wrong and be found out and shamed. Perhaps, for you, it's all of the above.

So let's cut to the chase and work through the most painless way of documenting skills, achievements and qualifications in a format that is readily accessible, and able to be repurposed when necessary.

Career transition consultant, Gary Henderson, from Audrey Page & Associates, suggests the best way to tackle the résumé project is to create, in an electronic word document, one master résumé which covers all there is to know about you. This will include education; all work experience including voluntary, project, part-time and community as well as full-time paid work; skills; all qualifications no matter how (seemingly) irrelevant to desired future directions; associations of which you are, or have been, a member; travel; hobbies; family and anything else which might be relevant to your ability to do future work.

Getting specific

From this master résumé, you will now be able to create role-specific résumés when you identify interesting positions. Read the position description or work brief carefully, and select only the most relevant information from your master document. Create a new résumé with the date and the name of the organisation and your own name as a file reference. Make sure the prioritising of the information in this document relates to the priorities within the description of the role for which you are applying or the project for which you are pitching.

When describing past work roles, write a brief summary organised into title, reporting to, responsibilities, and concrete achievements. This tailored résumé should run to no more than three A4 pages—if you can't elicit interest in a potential hirer by the end of the third page then there is little hope the fourth will set them on fire! When the tailored résumé is complete, don't just spell-check it—give it to someone you know who has a fine command of your mother tongue and ask them to check it for any literals, grammatical glitches or awkward phrasing. If they know you well they may also suggest any oversights in terms of relevant experience that you may have overlooked either due to forgetfulness or excess modesty.

When your application or proposal is complete don't just upload it to a job site or email it to the prospective hirer. You also need to print it, on good-quality paper, and mail it to the organisation concerned. In an age of email overload it is possible your email has been spammed, or deposited in a junk box, facing the sad and lonely fate of being automatically deleted when your targeted recipient boots off. Another advantage of using snail mail is that the rarity of post can actually make your offering stand out more than your competitors. And finally, the advice from most recruitment specialists—never fail to follow-up by phone to confirm your application has arrived, the name of the decision-maker, and when they, or a colleague, will respond.

It's old-fashioned, but it works.

The log book

List-makers are born, not created. You might be one, writing endless lists of clothes to pack, vegetables to buy, places you hope to visit, movies you are longing to see. Others seem to go through life on automatic pilot. It's a personal choice, but when seeking a really satisfying job, the log book is essential.

As you navigate your way through the maze of possible roles, required skills and attributes, companies and people and courses you may need along the way, you're unlikely to have a memory sufficient to hold all this data.

Treat yourself to a simple lever arch file with an index that allows you to sort your meaningful work search into the six Connecting your career dots classifications: sectors, organisations, roles, work arrangements, location and learning. Add one extra for contacts. Within these seven categories you can file all the information you amass, running an index up the front of each category so you can quickly locate useful contact details if and when necessary. Into this folder, you can also save a brief list of observations after informational interviews, formal job interviews, networking events or conferences, as well as all the fine print/detail of the skills you hope to add to your armoury. You can also use this folder as a job diary, with notes of meetings and phone calls as you work your way through your target job research.

Although getting organised is a pain in the butt and staying organised is even harder, once it's done, life becomes a whole lot simpler!

You've done it!

Your pitch was emailed, mailed, followed up by phone and to your delight and amazement they actually want to see you.

Help!

Another opportunity to be found wanting or, worse still, found out, has just loomed on the horizon . . .

Hugh Davies
A confident demeanour

Before the interview:

- Do some homework on what the work you are being interviewed for is about: what are the four or five key deliverables required (e.g. revenue growth, cost reduction, customer retention, quality, leadership of change, strategy formation).
- Then prepare a page under each deliverable and write up relevant achievements from your past: those things which you have delivered in former roles that relate directly to the deliverable of the new position.
- Next, work up some good questions to ask in that area of the new job.
- Work out well in advance what questions you will ask. Good questions reveal as much about your capabilities as do your own assertions and achievement stories.

... Networking helps those seeking work to understand what's out there. It's important that you know how to ask really good questions.

At the interview:

- Take the notes you have prepared—an interview is not a test of your memory.
- You will acquit yourself well if you display energy and enthusiasm in an interview: this is a large part of what a prospective hirer is going to be looking for. Technical skills and knowledge can be taught: enthusiasm and energy tends to come with (or not be found in) each individual.
- Do not try to 'manage' your body language—this is too hard in an interview unless you are a trained actor. Use the 'bum-wedge'

technique instead—place your backside firmly in the base of the chair—this will force your body forward so you will lean into the discussion, achieving a confident and engaged demeanor. It is hard to cross your arms across your chest in a defensive manner, or cross your legs in too much of a relaxed manner, with your bottom pushed back into the chair. Do this, and you can then forget about body language.

- Dress well (and suitably if you can find out beforehand the age, level of seniority of interviewer), take notes, look professional.
- Make sure your pre-interview notes are professionally laid out. You can then say, if appropriate, 'I haven't had time to offer all my thoughts/questions, so may I leave these with you?' This immediately raises the bar for most of the other candidates being considered by that organisation.

Remember, only 10 to 20 per cent of people get hired through the visible market which includes recruiters and online search engines. The other 80 per cent of hires come from networking and referrals (these can include research-driven conversations or informational interviews). Such networking helps those seeking work to understand what's out there. It's important that you know how to ask really good questions.

Hugh Davies is principal of career transition company, Macfarlan Lane <www.macfarlanlane.com.au>

A meeting of equals

Turn your interview into a meeting between two people who share a goal and who are motivated to explore how they can work together to get a job done in the best possible way.

—**Nick Corcodilos, Ask the Headhunter**

Once a job interview was a power play between a (more) powerful employer who would control the dialogue with the (less) powerful job applicant. Just as the predictable collar-and-tie, nine-to-five nature of many jobs has changed, so has the interview. It is now much more a 'conversation between equals' which aims to ascertain how well suited an organisation and an individual might be.

There are three phases involved in a successful interview; the preparation, the meeting and the follow-up. The preparation should take a while. This involves analysing the position description or the salient points in the advertisement/brief and creating four or five key contributors for the success of the appointment. These might include an understanding of the cost basis of a business, experience in people management and ability to deal at board level, or hands-on experience on the factory floor. You are identifying the critical performance areas required and then listing your relevant achievements against each one, as well as further questions to ask.

Hugh Davies believes you are there to win the job offer, but not necessarily to accept it. This you can decide away from the 'heat' of the table. Further interview tips are listed below.

Interview tips
from the top coaches

1. Prepare, prepare, prepare.
2. Dress smartly—this includes attention to shoes (shiny) hair (neat) grooming (tidy) personal hygiene (immaculate).
3. Arrive slightly early.
4. Remind yourself you are 'shopping' just as much as the interviewer. This is not the only work assignment in the world, you are here to learn more about it and it may or may not suit someone of your many talents.

5. Energy, enthusiasm and engagement cannot be faked. If you have selected the 'right' interview to attend, this will be your secret advantage.

6. Likewise with background knowledge. If you have been researching a specific type of work and know a lot about the industry, company and future trends, here comes your second standout advantage.

7. If you feel you need to try hard to impress, to be the kind of person the company might want to hire, then you won't be yourself. Do you really want to win work in an environment where, along with the pressures of day-to-day work, you will need to act as well?

8. It's entirely reasonable to ask about the selection process—how long, who is involved, whether there are follow-on interviews, how successful and unsuccessful candidates will be informed. It's not just reasonable—it's your right.

Based on the BTSO (Blow their socks off) approach used in coaching by career consultants of Macfarlan Lane
<www.macfarlanlane.com.au>

Lastly, the follow-up. It's a good idea to write a note acknowledging the opportunity to discuss the role and thanking the interviewer for their time. You may also wish to reinforce your enthusiasm for the role if you want to be considered a serious candidate. Email it for speed—and mail it for courtesy.

Handling knockbacks

So you got a knockback. You thought the interview went really well and they loved you—and your extensive experience. But now you've received the briefest of emails (not even a phone call!) to say another candidate was successful and they hope you will be too—in your future endeavours, elsewhere!

The nerve, the pain, the humiliation.

You hope their factory burns down or their selected candidate fails spectacularly in the role which should have been yours.

It's worse than being dumped at the Year 12 high school formal— at least you had your whole life ahead of you then!

Okay, okay, it is disappointing. You win some, you lose some and nowhere is it written that you will necessarily like the losing part.

But all is not lost.

You've just had a great opportunity to not only practise your interview skills but also to learn how one company operates, how they recruit and how your particular bundle of attributes suited the advertised role.

What to do? Write it down! Take the time, while the memory (and yes, the hurt) is still fresh and commit to paper the areas where you believe you performed well in the interview, those on which you felt shaky and a few dot points of skills you might need to acquire to do better next time.

And yes, unlike the formal, there will be repeat performances ...

Chapter wrap

Before leaving behind the wisdom of Bolles, Corcodilos and Ibarra, let's reconsider their strategies for selling your talents and take a lesson from each. From Bolles, take persistence and the advice that it may be the one thing that separates you from the pack when it matters most. From Corcodilos, take the importance of avoiding 'interviewitis', deciding to only tackle those roles which have a strong and sensible match to the work you do or want to do. And finally, from Ibarra, take the strong message that we need to get started now, to act immediately, if we are to change our working lives.

Connecting the career dots

Trike man, Alan Maxwell, made the move from employee to consultant five years ago. His passion for motorbikes was the genesis of a tourism business which he and his wife, Joh, run in their spare time. The growth of this business has seen the need to employ two part-time drivers and a manager. Alan uses his original IT skills during his daytime consultancy work and is developing tourism knowledge in his new sector. He is hoping his own business will eventually replace his role as a consultant.

Fiona Corr's approach to career change has been through higher education. Her original degree which provided the skills for a career as a concert performer included a teaching qualification. After years of teaching music, Fiona once again attended university, where she is currently writing a PhD thesis on children and learning. Fiona needed to sell her talents to the PhD selection panel and this meant thinking on her feet and having the confidence to respond directly to a particularly tough line of questioning.

8

Skilling up

Popular media seems to enjoy nothing better than the suggestion someone has 'made it' in their chosen field. Yet often the subject comes across as smug, self-satisfied, even boring. That's probably because the human condition is all about striving for something better. The same can be said of our skills. When we rest easy, believing we have peaked at our game, whatever that game may be, we expose ourselves to the dangers of complacency, or worse. We simply cannot hope to remain workplace-relevant unless we are prepared to engage in ongoing professional development. This requires an audit of our current skills—and those which will be needed for future work, including any planned changes of sector or role. Once identified, these skills can be readily upgraded by researching the most appropriate education or training and where or how it can be undertaken. Claiming ownership of this need for ongoing professional development is the first step.

> *To grow is to go beyond what you are today.*
> *Stand up as yourself.*
> *Do not imitate.*
> *Do not pretend to have achieved your goal, and do not try to cut corners.*
> *Just try to grow.*
> **—Svami Prajnanpad, Hindu spiritual master 1891–1974**

Why bother?

Successful organisations reinvent themselves continually. In *The Empty Raincoat*, futurist Charles Handy describes this process as a sigmoid curve. This elongated S-shaped curve can best be summarised as the ability, while the corporate star is still soaring, to realise the need for a new way of doing things as well as the ability to identify a new way forward and implement that new direction before your first modus operandi has peaked or begun to wane.

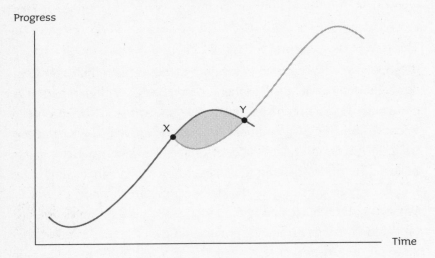

Using the analogy of the sigmoid curve for individual careers is extremely useful. This concept of seeing the future *before it arrives* encourages us to remain workplace-relevant and to continue to work productively and enjoyably for the foreseeable future. Thus, if one old way of working starts to wane, we already have 'lift off' occurring due to our new initiatives.

Your career trajectory

The analogy of a company's strategic planning provides a very useful starting point when looking at our own career trajectories and skills development. We readily accept the idea that companies need to remain up-to-date and that to do so they must invest in technologies, knowledge, new methods and ongoing development of their human resources. We, too, need to replenish our skills on an ongoing basis.

If we are prepared to understand and accept that future 'jobs' are shrinking for *all* workers, but future 'work possibilities' are expanding, then we are free to rethink our work selves as businesses of one. These solo operations have the same needs as those companies which employ hundreds or thousands of employees, the only difference being the scale. In short, if we want to stay ahead of the pack, we need to invest time, money and energy in our personal 'work' product. This means we need to become involved in a process of lifelong learning. This is the exact opposite of a frenzied period of retraining driven by the desire to get a new position, after which we relax, 'secure' in the new role. Re-skilling is an ongoing project which, tackled sensibly, can lead to a much more productive way of living and, better still, a more satisfying level of work engagement. It's not so much about work 'til you drop; rather, learn until you lie down.

Les Bartlett:
Les builds an oven

Mum and Dad organised my first job in a bank when I was fifteen. It offered good holidays, good money and superannuation, which they considered important. I lasted two or three years and then I did wildlife photography for three years with my uncle. I gained my matriculation as a mature-age student when I was 24 and met my wife, Judith, who had three boys. I studied further and worked in teaching, rehabilitation and health and safety in Brisbane. In 1995 my marriage broke up. I was 43 and had no ties so I escaped into taxi driving for three years before I found Crystal Waters. It's an intentional community of about 640 acres near Maleny behind the Sunshine Coast in Queensland. The original owner of the property wanted people to share the land. Residents can own an acre lot and the rest belongs to the community. The idea was that people would earn their living from this land but this hasn't caught on yet, so most go off to a day job. It's a lovely place to live, a rural area at the head of the Mary River, with no cats or dogs, so lots of birds and small mammals. It gives me the sort of quiet I was seeking in my life.

When I was living in Brisbane I knew I wanted something different but didn't know what it was. My main move was to break from the nine-to-five mainstream 'working for the man' stuff. I now have the freedom to focus my work ethically, morally and spiritually. I believe work is the way you interact with your community. So in 2001 I built a community wood-fired oven at Crystal Waters.

I was trapped for 30 years and I'm so glad I've been able to make this transition. It came about because I focused more on my inner development . . .

It was hard getting the right design but I finally located one in the United States—an Alan Scott design—by searching on the internet. James, a friend of my sons, came to teach us how to make sourdough bread. I really didn't know I would become a baker but I'm passionate about it now. I was trapped for 30 years and I'm so glad I've been able to make this transition. It came about because I focused more on my inner development and let the external stuff happen around me. I didn't sit down and furiously plan, but worked inside and let the outside stuff gather its own momentum. Now I cut the wood, make the bread and have a direct relationship with the people who buy it. We hand-mix stone-ground local flour. I met my partner, Lesley, through this community and she has played an important part in the business and my spiritual process.

The bakery has made money from the first day we baked bread, but this is because of the low investment and extremely low overheads. It's an advantage of living in Crystal Waters. I was able to use their commercial kitchen initially before I obtained a food licence and I am paying a peppercorn rent compared to the normal commercial lease.

I live a fairly meagre existence and I have deliberately structured it like that. I only bake one or two days a week to supply local folk and a market. I could bake a lot more but I'm trying to find a balance between the amount of time I spend baking and doing other things I consider important. I learnt a lot from James and through trial and error and extensive reading so I now feel I can call myself a baker. This has taken nearly nine years. I used to get my identity from my work. Now my work is a reflection of the deeper part of me.

I really admire younger folk who move into this sort of lifestyle while their kids are young. They have so much more at risk. It was easier for me. By the time I finally started making a move I was divorced and my kids had left home. I didn't have to consider anyone else; I could live off odd jobs. My sons have also been an inspiration to me. Justin has started his own cheesery recently, Damon works from home on local environmental consultancies and structures his work to suit his family, and Conrad put himself through a double degree at uni so he could be a forensic scientist like *Quincy* but after interviews with the police and health departments decided that if he had to work in those sorts of cultures he would rather make furniture from recycled timber—so he did. I'm lucky to be surrounded by such inspiring people.

Les Bartlett owns and runs the Crystal Waters Sourdough Bakery
‹www.sourdough.com/bakery/crystal-waters›

The (training) buck stops with you

So how do you start the process of skilling up?

Your first step is the acceptance that you will never have 'made' it and that professional development is an ongoing, not finite, process.

The minute you start to feel you are 'successful' is when you need most to reassess how the world of work has shifted around you and to ask yourself what you need to do to most effectively meet its new requirements. Like it or not, life is a whole lot easier when we understand we are all merely a work-in-progress. This requires a wholehearted acceptance of the ownership of your ongoing work relevance—and the dumping of expectations that your employer, your immediate boss, your colleagues, your family or anyone else should provide the necessary training framework or support.

It's not unreasonable to expect on-the-job training, during work hours, funded by your employer. It's just not that likely to happen anymore. Gillian Considine, Research Manager at the Workplace Research Centre, Faculty of Economics and Business, University of Sydney, notes a shifting of responsibility for workplace training, suggesting employers are more likely to provide training and developmental opportunities to selected senior employees, but rarely to the low-skilled. Employee participation in training has increased (some 89 per cent of employees have accessed training in recent years) but this is often self-motivated and more than likely to be paid for by the employees themselves.

So waiting for your employer to offer training means you are immediately putting yourself behind nearly nine out of ten workers when it comes to skills enhancement.

Skills defined

We often hear people discussing other people's 'skill sets', but are rarely offered a clear definition which explains differences between skills that cross occupations and those that are specific to a role or task. To stay skilled up thus becomes a difficult project if we do not have a clear understanding of which skills are the most important to gain and retain. Our skills can (and if we're lucky, will) change and develop a lot during the course of our lives, either from our own active intervention, or external factors, perhaps good or bad luck. Consider the example of Olympic medal winner, Cathy Freeman, whose early work skills were to run, very fast. Time has seen her acquire many other skills, including managing her running career as a business, becoming a spokesperson and an interviewee, a television presenter and, more recently, a fundraiser.

Work skills belong to one of five different categories:

- transferable (or generic)
- industry- or task-specific
- people (personal and interpersonal)
- promotional
- technological

These categories are not rigid compartments. They do, however, offer five different frameworks with which to test your different abilities in order to highlight potential gaps in expertise, or fun things you might like to learn which will help you move in new directions at a later date.

Transferable skills

When it comes to the search for meaningful work, the concept of transferable skills is simultaneously one of the most heartening—and potentially misleading—of all. Heartening, in that we all have a store of useful skills which may be applied across a range of occupations. But the danger is that we may be lulled into thinking that the combination of our innate talents and these basic skills will allow us to try our hands at a range of different occupations and that we will succeed on the basis of these alone. This is highly unlikely. There's a lot more to most employment than just these abilities.

In job-seeking parlance and on recruitment websites, there are five commonly listed skills that are completely transferable from workplace to workplace. These are:

- communication
- research and planning
- human relations
- organisation, management and leadership
- work survival

A visit to the About.com career-planning website will give you access to a worksheet that allows you to rate your transferable skills.

Other perspectives on transferable skills

Gillian Considine offers a different way of understanding your potentially transferable skills, defined through research as:

- cognitive
- technical
- behavioural

The cognitive skills include literacy, numeracy and problem-solving. Technical refers to the underlying cognitive capacity required to develop these cognitive skills and relates to the specific skills (including knowledge) required to complete the work, for example typing, electrical wiring, driving or surgery. Behavioural broadly encompasses values and attitudes—the 'work ethic' issues. The behavioural skills are harder to define because what employers want in employees may not be reasonable and/or achievable in particular workplaces. For example, deference and/or compliance with authority (which most employers are after) is difficult and/or unreasonable to demonstrate as an employee if workplace practices are poor, unfair or exploitative. There's also a lot of debate about whether or not 'values' are a skill (trainable) or a personal attribute (inherent).

When considering transferable skills, Gillian Considine believes work seekers might think of their technical skills and then consider the underlying cognitive skills that enable them to demonstrate those technical skills. For example, many technical skills are based on transferable cognitive skills such as problem-solving, attention to detail, speed and accuracy, and the capacity to learn.

Yet another definition of transferable skills comes from American author Richard Bolles, who shares a practical framework grouping skills into one of three categories: those with which we manipulate data, relate to people or handle things. Yet regardless of our preferred understanding of 'transferable', these skills, on their own, are not useful indicators of our ability to perform any specific roles.

Gary Henderson
Not what you have, but how you've used it

ask *the* expert

In his work as a career transition consultant, Gary Henderson avoids the term 'skills' when helping clients seeking new roles. He believes that a focus on skills is far too narrow and that there is often a tendency to confuse skills with personal attributes. Instead, he prefers the term 'capabilities', which he describes as the abilities that enable you to get certain jobs done. When working with clients, he suggests they look back over recent work experience—say the past ten years—and the jobs they have done. He asks them to consider their achievements using the STAR model—Situation, Task, Action, Result.

A list of five to ten such achievements will quickly reveal the capabilities and personal attributes which enabled the worker to achieve the desired outcome. This is where the concept of the 'transfer' is useful, says Gary. But the transfer is not in the moving of a skill from one role to the next. The important 'transference' is into the potential client or employer's mind. 'If she got that result in a previous engagement, then that can be repeated in the future. If she did that before, she can do that for my business!'

One example Gary cites of this process in action is a former client's challenge relating to the poor sales performance of a regional Asian office. Saul, the client concerned, was able to identify the underperforming staff, and replace these salespeople with more suitable and proactive employees, to achieve a revenue turnaround. The client could discern his *capabilities* which included strategic thinking, an understanding of the local sales culture, an ability to select and manage the right recruitment expertise, and to successfully induct the new staff.

Personal *attributes* included a cool head, the courage to take tough decisions and to remove staff who were not suitable and to quickly fill these positions with the right people. Saul could probably have listed about 140 'transferable' skills he has gained during his 25 years of work, but these skills, however impressive, are, in isolation, rather meaningless. They also fail to demonstrate clearly to a potential employer, colleague or business partner the *way* Saul might utilise his many skills. A situation which has been well handled cannot fail to demonstrate relevant capabilities in action. At the end of the day, these are the ones that will carry you forward.

Gary Henderson is a career transition consultant at Audrey Page & Associates
<www.audreypage.com.au>

Industry- or task-specific skills

While industry-specific skills, for insiders, are easy to identify, most workers do not keep up with new developments in their own industry let alone understand skills in other industries. Many workers toil long hours and crave rest and recreation rather than a round or two of personal development in their downtime. The best solution is to try to include the professional development within your working hours and to try to ensure training is part of any future work assignment.

Those whose work involves attending conferences, frequent meetings with challenging and interesting colleagues or training and further educational opportunities are indeed privileged. They are able to remain industry-relevant at someone else's expense. Recent research from careerone.com.au indicates in many cases a majority of workers rate training and/or learning opportunities as more important than salary considerations. For those who are not being offered such opportunities, there is still a need to understand where the industry in which they are currently employed is heading. For instance, is it a sunset industry? A recent example of such decline was the decision by General Motors (GM) in 2009 to cease production of Pontiac cars. So if your expertise was Pontiac-specific your work prospects at GM were looking rather dim. The upside is that there will always be Pontiac aficionados. So if your skills are in the repairing or maintaining of what has now become a scarce and highly prized automobile, then you just may be able to name your price on the market!

One of the easiest ways to stay abreast of industry directions, practices and required skills is by reading trade journals. Regardless of profession or trade, there exists a journal, usually print and electronic, which covers the topical issues. An online search is probably the best way to track down the most relevant publication for your sector, but a visit to the local library or a look at the Yahoo!7 business news listing could also prove productive. (See the Notes and Resources section for the web address.) You need to keep up with current industry news, personalities and happenings, as well as new ways of working in that industry, so you can form a picture of what might be coming—well ahead of the pack. It is this industry prescience or forward thinking that is guaranteed to differentiate your approach when seeking a new job, role or project.

Consider, also, the abundance of local industry organisations. Are you a member of any? Do you attend events or meetings? Have you considered becoming an office holder? Such organisations are often the first to receive and share professional development opportunities. Why would you deliberately cut yourself out of the loop by refusing to join?

People skills

Whether they are called people, personal, or interpersonal skills, we all recognise the possession of such skills as a great attribute. But what do good people skills really involve, apart from being a likeable type? And if we don't have such skills naturally, how can we go about acquiring them? How, also, can we objectively judge our own people skills when one person's idea of socially awkward might be seen by another as a sensitive listener?

People skills remain the most subjective area of our expertise and so are extremely difficult to improve if you feel this is necessary. If you wish to consider the strength of your ability to relate to others with confidence, a good starting point is a very old book—*How to Win Friends and Influence People* by Dale Carnegie. Don't laugh—it still makes lot of sense and offers some great tips.

Promotional skills

Selling yourself and your talents is a necessary evil, whether you are an employee, a contractor or a consultant. Advertising and marketing experts know only too well that it's of little use having the greatest product on the face of the earth if no one knows about it. Similarly, you may have the greatest range of skills known to humankind, but if potential employers or work colleagues don't know about them, it won't matter a toss. The simple truth is that you need to market your skills in order to sell your services. For those who develop a rash at the mere mention of self-promotion, the best approach is to embrace the concept of the Brand You marketing campaign, understanding that it will be based on *factual* evidence of your aptitude. You can then apply yourself to it with single-minded zeal, comfortable in the knowledge you are not selling bullshit to baffle brains but promoting an entirely worthwhile cause. It makes a difference.

Technological skills

Futurist and business forecaster Phil Ruthven grew up in a work world of typewriters, overhead projectors and personal secretaries. He now works in a small office complex utilising the latest technologies to communicate with branch offices of IBISWorld in the United States and Shanghai. He is living evidence that Baby Boomers and beyond not only 'get' technology—they drive the technology decisions of small, medium and large companies. Ruthven warns, 'Communication technology is not an option. It is a life support skill as important as reading, writing and arithmetic.'

The need for current technological skills has been covered in Chapter 2, but it is important to reiterate that a working understanding of computers, including word processing, databases, spreadsheets, email and internet is no longer a handy thing. It is imperative if you wish to operate 'in the loop' both at work and at home, during the coming century. At the most basic level, if there is an essential requirement for an internet application for a position you want, if you can't manage the upload of your vital documents, you will never even make the list of applicants.

The good news is that it is easier to acquire computer skills than it ever has been, and it's becoming far more affordable. Federal government programs mean technology is now heavily subsidised for the aged and/or economically or physically disadvantaged—including subsidies for home internet connections (see the Notes and Resources section for the web address). There are fewer and fewer barriers to most Australians accessing and using the internet as frequently as they like.

Doreen Spurdens:
A *passport to the world*

I've experienced three main careers in my life so far. I completed A Levels at secondary school in the north of England and was then faced with the traditional trifecta of choice for girls: teacher, nurse or secretary. I chose the third and my typing and shorthand skills have stood me in good stead over the years. My main motivation has

---

always been travel and I worked in Germany and South Africa before marrying Tim [see Tim Spurdens' profile in Chapter 5] in the early 1970s and heading off around the world. When we reached Australia we decided to stay. I've always had good English skills, so when a position came up as a publications officer, I grabbed it. This involved writing, editing and interviewing for the staff magazine and I loved it.

However, I didn't enjoy the office politics and so went freelance for fifteen years, enjoying the freedom tremendously. I felt I was getting stale but in 1999 two things happened to change that. My mother, for whom I was the main caregiver, passed away and I turned 50. Call it a midlife crisis if you like, but for the first time in a while I was free of responsibility. I saw an advertisement in a local paper for TESL—training to teach English as a Second Language—which I undertook part time for three months. Up to now I'd been a behind-the-scenes type of person, so standing up in front of a class was a major challenge.

> *Work isn't just a means to an end to get money to live. It gets you into areas where you can learn more.*

I'd also been studying Indonesian language and belonged to an Indonesian association. I was keen to live and work overseas and quickly realised that teaching English was a passport to the world. I searched the internet and found a job in Bandung, the third largest city in Java. I deliberately chose it for the mountain location as I don't like heat. This was a major step into the unknown for me as Tim stayed home. I worked in Bandung for ten months. It was very tough and I felt very isolated. Phone calls were prohibitively expensive, email erratic and I was disappointed to never become very proficient in the language. My salary was about $AUD200 a month. Living on the outskirts of town, I was occasionally fearful, but enjoyed a couple of wonderful friendships with local people.

By the time I returned to Australia Tim also had itchy feet and he'd been checking out the Australian Volunteers International [AVI] website. Next thing I knew AVI called to offer me a teaching position in Laos. I was unsure where Laos was, but said yes anyway. Tim was supposed to be a 'supporting partner' but soon he, too, was teaching. Again the living allowance was small, but we had little opportunity to spend, so it was a break-even situation.

Money has never been all that important to me. It's very liberating to find out how much you can achieve on less money and to visit developing countries and realise how local people can get by on very little. By contrast Australians are caught up in consumerism and miss the simpler pleasures and importance of personal relationships. I now know I can have a good life without major income and this is very liberating.

Our volunteering has been an experiment and to a certain extent we've burnt our bridges. It would be difficult to re-establish myself as a freelance writer but I have a very sustainable career in teaching English. I keep my skills up by taking short courses and maintaining my interest in the wider world. Work isn't just a means to an end to get money to live. It gets you into areas where you can learn more.

Doreen Spurdens is a writer and volunteer teacher

Next step skills

To undertake her voluntary teaching, Doreen found it necessary to learn both Indonesian and to do a formal ESL course. Which skills will take you forward into your next career or work assignment? Take the time to consider the listed skills in Table 8.1, filling in the middle column with those you currently possess. Then use the third column to note the skills you wish you had, those you feel could stand some strengthening and those that just sound like fun.

Table 8.1 Your skills

Skill type	Your current repertoire	Skills to acquire
Transferable		
Industry- or task-specific		
People (personal and interpersonal)		
Promotional		
Technological		
Other		

The landscape of learning

Now you have a clearer idea of the nature of the skills you wish to acquire, how and where do you get them? Traditionally our learning took place outside the home, in an institute which was age-specific; a kindergarten, primary school, secondary school, technical college or university. A lucky few had this education supplemented with workplace training. Today the flexibility in delivery of education and training means there is a bewildering array of possibilities for anyone wishing to upgrade their skills. You might achieve this through home study, distance learning, online or weekend courses, an apprenticeship, a weekend workshop within or outside your place of work. You might join a professional association for the value of the courses it offers, or seek out adult education classes for a taste of a new subject which seems of interest. Or you might approach a bricks-and-mortar institution such as a TAFE or university to commence a certificate, diploma or degree course.

Your current work and family commitments might steer you towards the options of distance or online learning on offer from most educational providers. Whichever way you decide to go, the fundamental decisions you will need to make are:

- Is the content and quality of instruction in line with your requirements?
- Is the course affordable both financially and in terms of your time?
- Will the qualification be respected and/or recognised by potential employers/hirers?
- Does the course excite you?

If you have found a training program or educational course which satisfies the above four questions, you'd be mad not to sign up!

Overcoming obstacles

There are many reasons why people aren't engaged in continuing personal development and not all of them are of their own making. It may be that you are working so many hours to cover current commitments that there is simply no time or money left to invest in further training. Other reasons may be related to a lack of education or experience, you may think you are too old, or suffer from other cultural or medical disadvantages. You may also suffer from low self-esteem and believe that you won't qualify for any particular course on offer. None of these obstacles are insurmountable. The first step is to identify the type of development you would like to undertake and then locate the student services officer at the institution or organisation concerned. There are usually subsidies, hardship payments and special support for people keen to improve their lot in life, but lacking the initial resources.

Chapter wrap

'Why bother?' was the first question asked in the chapter. Surely life is demanding enough without the need to start studying after a long day at work and a hectic family meal? It's a fair question. And the answer is similarly straightforward, if we go back to the first line of the quote at the beginning of the chapter: 'To grow is to go beyond what you are today.' It is only through ongoing personal growth that we can progress in our private and public lives. By being open to what the world is trying to tell—and teach—us we will go forward. Our ongoing personal development does not have to include onerous formal study tasks. Nowadays there are plenty of other ways to to grow through learning. What it does require, however, is a willing heart and an open mind.

Connecting the career dots

Les Bartlett managed to cover all six categories in the Connecting your career dots grid, but in a more organic way, both literally and as a work-seeking strategy. His move from full-time paid employment to running his own bakery was triggered by a change in location to the intentional community of Crystal Waters and driven by a desire to do something for this community. He has learnt how to bake, and researched and read widely, but is keeping his business in check to maintain his preferred work–life balance.

After leaving full-time employment, Doreen Spurdens added to her writing skills with a TESL qualification, which, combined with Indonesian language skills, gave her a new direction in volunteering. She has built upon her teaching skills with a second assignment in Laos and continues to embrace both formal and informal learning opportunities.

9

Be your own boss

Many people dream of becoming their own boss. Some hope their business will be a world-beater, leading to fame and fortune. Others hope it will deliver a secure income, job satisfaction and a relatively peaceful existence. Realistically, with 93 per cent of Australian businesses in the 'micro' category, your chance of starting the next Microsoft is a long shot. Believing that running your own business will lead to security and a quiet life is also a furphy. Running your own business normally involves long (often unpaid) hours, hard work and high risk. It can, however, be incredibly satisfying and offer the most meaningful work you will ever experience.

What it takes

Do you have what it takes to run your own business? And if so, what will it look, feel and smell like? Perhaps you've had a great business idea for a while and believe that this is something you are keen to explore sooner rather than later. There are three ways to become your own boss; buying an established business, buying a franchised business or creating your own startup company. This chapter considers the qualities business owners need to possess and some of the challenges they will face. It also offers resources you can use to test your business ambitions, access specific training and groom yourself for business success. It does not tell you how to become a successful business operator. The Notes and Resources section lists useful references for this bigger ambition.

The aim is to assist you to consider your suitability as a business owner/operator, and to achieve one of two goals. It will either dissuade you from this calling because you are simply not suited to the long hours, single-minded commitment and myriad thankless tasks you will need to perform along the way. Or it will encourage you to do your homework, test your business proposition and then simply go for it—and have the ride of your life.

Shanghai startup

A retired engineer, Guan Tongxian was 59 when he started up a port machinery business in Shanghai. At a time when many others thought he should be seeking a quieter life away from the workplace, Guan accessed government funding to establish the Shanghai Zhenhua Port Machinery Company which now hires 30,000 workers and has a capitalisation of US$450 million.

It's easy to be overwhelmed by such a huge startup success story. But it's worthwhile remembering that Guan, too, needed to overcome barriers—in his case perceptions about the ability of older workers. Maybe your great startup idea is delivering hand-baked cakes to local factories with a staff of just one—you! But you are scared. Guan's story serves to highlight the fact that all businesses have barriers to overcome, regardless of their size or market. These barriers may be financial, political, legal, cultural, driven by peer group pressure, or your nerves. They are not a reason to resist the self-employment road; they are, however, points which need to be addressed before taking the leap.

As the world of paid employment changes dramatically, so does the landscape of business startups. If work is a way of expressing yourself, running your own enterprise has to be the ultimate form of career expression.

But is it for you?

The time is right

There has never been a better time to start your own business. In fact one in three Australians now view running a business as a more attractive career path than being a wage or salary earner. It's becoming easier than ever to reshape your core competencies into an attractive, marketable package with an ABN (Australian Business Number) attached and let more of the profits stay in *your* pocket rather than flowing to an employer's bottom line. Political and technological change has caused the dissolution of the formal workplace as well as trade barriers and national borders. The removal of these barriers gives smaller entrepreneurs the opportunity to move (literally and figuratively) much more freely into the space previously dominated by large, long-established institutions. As we saw in Chapter 2, this shift in power was documented in *The Cluetrain Manifesto*, a collection of observations created collaboratively by four tech-savvy American observers. Their manifesto confirmed for Craig Newmark the rationale behind his creation of the online community known as craigslist. This website has been valued at up to $6 billion but, according to the owner, it's simply not for sale.

Big dollars, but a business which started in the owner's living room, using inexpensive technology harnessing the power of an idea—a network of people helping each other out—matched to a perceived need—the need for an independent classifieds website which was not corrupted by a corporation's desire to make profits.

Natasha Boyd:
By the book

After teaching for eleven years in the secondary school system I decided I was burning out so my partner and I made a tree change to a school near Kyneton in rural Victoria where I taught Year 11 and 12 students. But even here I experienced burnout caused by a heavy workload and parent politics. I loved teaching the kids, but needed to learn how to switch off. I decided I needed to change careers and considered a bed & breakfast or a chocolate shop.

A friend suggested a bookstore. But country towns such as the one we were living in can usually only support one such shop, so I worked in a chain bookstore for four months. I told the owner that I wanted to open my own shop—and asked him to give me one shift to see how well I could work. I was lucky—he showed me behind the scenes. Although his store was a franchise, I thought my own ideas for a 'community' bookshop would work better in an independent bookstore.

During a few evenings over a period of two weeks I took a Council of Adult Education (CAE) course entitled *Running Your Own Bookshop*. Here I learnt about Leading Edge, a network for independent booksellers which includes a buying group, a catalogue and incentives. I also did a lot of research online, contacted the Australian Booksellers Association, visited many bookstores and asked the managers about their inventory management. This, as well as the CAE course, meant I could make an informed choice about how to run our store, which software package we would use and any necessary training.

Next I needed a logo and found a graphic designer and experienced website designer recommended to me by a great business mentor who had opened her own beauty salon the year prior. It was all falling into place. I resigned from teaching, took my long-service payout and used the money to go to Africa for a seven-week honeymoon, before returning to Melbourne and getting married—slightly back-to-front, I guess. If the bookshop hadn't gone ahead, we planned to return to Africa to work as volunteers in schools there, although my new husband, Mark, was a little hesitant about this until our trip confirmed how worthwhile it would be.

... life changes, people change, and I am glad, inspired by my husband, I made this change, took a risk and did something I love.

Upon our return in 2007 I worked at my old school part-time until the end of the second term when we found shop premises in Essendon. The location is not ideal but the rent was reasonable and this gave us three years to decide if the business would work. We opened in mid-August. Word of mouth has worked very well for us. When we did our business plan I didn't realise schools would be so important. They have come to us—particularly the library network. We run five adult book clubs, a fortnightly kids' storytime and offer workshops for parents to understand childhood literacy. It's the teacher experience kicking in. We have one year left on the lease and aim to move to a higher traffic area—we knew we needed to be in a location where there was a bank, bakery—people's daily shopping needs. But if we'd started there the rent would have killed us.

We didn't borrow from the bank to finance the business. We used our savings and went back to living on one salary. People can get into too much debt not knowing if they will like the business they've invested in. We certainly made sacrifices and I don't think I could have done it without the support of my husband, father and mother. When I became a teacher I thought I'd be a teacher forever. I thought it was my calling and what I was good at. But life changes, people change, and I am glad, inspired by my husband, I made this change, took a risk and did something I love. Running a bookshop is a lot of work, but a different kind of stress to teaching. In the end what I love is that I get to talk with great people about books.

Natasha Boyd is co-owner of Bookbonding

Business in Australia

To understand the context of small business in Australia today, visit the website of the Australian Bureau of Statistics (ABS). The ABS is a good friend to all business owners, but particularly to those starting their feasibility research. Here, at no cost, you can find an extraordinary repository of data which will enable you to measure and assess the opportunity you are pursuing, both before and during your business operation. According to the ABS, in June 2007 there were 2,011,770 actively trading businesses in Australia; approximately one business for every ten individuals. Nearly 60 per cent (1,171,832) of these businesses were non-employing and a whopping 93 per cent were termed micro-businesses—those which are either non-employing or employ between one and four people. Business survival rates are surprisingly high, especially for those businesses which have been around for ten or twenty years or more. But whilst the sheer number of fellow Australians starting up a business might give you heart, it is the industry-specific information which will give you the contextual understanding you need for your proposed venture, particularly in regard to your potential customer base, their demographics and geographical location.

Professor John English
Becoming a band leader—good reasons to establish your own business

1. professional independence
2. financial independence
3. substantial financial rewards (to create wealth)
4. the intrinsic value in pursuing a trade or craft and the personal satisfaction that comes from doing it really well

---

5. the satisfaction that comes from the process of building a business and the pathway to fulfil that kind of dream

Good reasons not to run your own show
1. Frustration with current employment. If you choose self-employment you may end up with five or six bosses and can end up hating your business just as much as you hated your job, but with the added problem that you can't quit.
2. Your personality—some people are simply not emotionally suited to running their own business.
3. Lack of proficiency in skills and/or experience required for a particular type of business.
4. You can lose everything you have—including the wife/husband and kids.

Most common mistakes people make in their own business
1. (Not) knowing what your market is. Very few people fully and totally understand the point of view of their customer. 'I know it will sell' is said way too often. Business owners need to put themselves in the shoes of their customer in order to deeply understand the subtle characteristics of what people really want. These finer nuances might create your competitive advantage instead of having to fall back and compete on price.
2. Not understanding the full gamut of what is needed to become operational. You are a bandleader requiring many different elements (people, premises, processes) to sing the same song.
3. Many people seem to manage businesses with up to five employees—but fail to make the transition from a one-person business to becoming an effective manager.
4. Not understanding the financial implications, specifically how many dollars are needed to open doors and get going. Ongoing

cash flow is a major issue. People often think rapid growth solves all problems. But growth consumes cash—it doesn't produce it.

Will your idea work?
You can research something to death and never know the answer, so just try it.

And know there are ways to minimise investment loss upfront. You might consider starting on a smaller scale and ways of minimising cash flow.

Or try a portfolio approach, trialling two or three projects and don't put a lot of money into each one.

Remember, though, that people who lack courage to get started might not be good at being self-employed. There are plenty of procrastinators; they are waiting because they are never going to do it.

Being self-employed is the hardest way in the world to make a living.

In 1984 John ('Jack') English wrote How to Organise and Operate a Small Business in Australia. *Twenty-five years later this small business 'bible' has sold 250,000 copies and is about to hit its eleventh edition.*

Why go there?

In his years of teaching and writing about running businesses, Jack English has developed two very different forms of business satisfaction. The first is derived from a business in which you can develop your craft and showcase your talents, be they sculpting, forensic accounting or panelbeating. The lure of your own business is based on the chance to show the world what you do well—and how *very* well you do it. The second form of satisfaction is based on the actual process of building and running a business. The thrill is in the chase, and not the nature of the catch.

There are those amongst us who are born entrepreneurs—I know of one such young man, Jesse, who is aged seventeen, but who already has a patent pending for a business tool. If this idea doesn't work he plans to come up with another one. He wants to run a business; to take an idea and build processes that will lead to profit. It is the mechanics of business that interest Jesse—the stock inventory, sales cycles, marketing initiatives and customer service fascinate him the most. Interestingly, these critical components of business are often the aspects which most frustrate the more purist craftspeople, who are happiest when locked away creating a masterpiece while someone else takes on the troublesome tasks of promoting, shipping and selling their work.

Knowing which of these two 'types' you are is a critical and fundamental first step towards understanding the nature of the enterprise you will lead. It also helps you define your optimal business activity and scale. If you are a craftsperson, it will encourage you to consider the options of remaining a small-scale artisan, or, if a larger volume enterprise is your desire, how to hire people with complementary skills.

Entrepreneur or technician?

If the actual running of the business is your first love, you may find your attributes match those of an entrepreneur. If the process of creating a product or delivering a service is more important, your attitude may be more in tune with that of a technician.

Understanding this distinction is another way of clarifying the skills your business will need in order to survive. This is well documented by Michael Gerber in his best-selling recipe for business survival, *The E Myth Revisited*. Gerber refers to the three critical roles within a business—entrepreneur, sales and technical—and notes that most small businesses start because a technician has a dream. And they fail because no one is minding the strategic and sales functions! It's impossible to be all things to all people on a personal, let alone a business, level. The smartest thing any budding business owner can do is to fully explore how they will make up for their own shortfalls within the business, *before* they open their doors.

Tim Terry:
Underground mushroom man

I've been a farmer all my life. I started on my dad's property in northern Tasmania where we had sheep, cattle and pigs and grew poppies, potatoes, peas, wheat and barley. It was my job to cut the rushes, which only grew because it was so wet. I fixed the problem by doing some training in the UK and becoming an underground land draining specialist. This was 30 years ago, and this skill led to a contracting business which grew into my livelihood for 25 years.

All wisdom to my father who had three sons and decided to split the farm ten to fifteen years ago while everything was still amicable. Then he went fishing and we went farming.

I, too, was fishing with a friend for mako sharks when he said, 'Have you heard about truffles?' I hadn't but wondered, given that Tasmania is the same latitude as France, why no one in Australia had done this before. My mate did further research and we decided truffle farming was worth a try. He started a company from which we bought our trees and on 18 June 1999 Australia's first black truffle was harvested on our farm. I realised that, at the time of year we produced, there were no truffles in season elsewhere in the world so this presented a niche market opportunity.

In 1999 we produced just a handful. I decided we needed to get bigger in order to commercialise and so created a prospectus for investors, something totally out of character with what I'd dealt with before. When the tax office came to discuss the business they thought the truffles were chocolates, as did the town planners.

This was the level of understanding of the truffle industry.

... but the real way you learn all these things is through experience. I like learning from mistakes.

There were a lot of skeptics but as we produced more truffles there was strong media coverage and interest from all around the world. But we couldn't just deliver once. We would need a continuity of high-quality product and so the family—my wife, Adele, and two children—supported my intention to increase our land to its current 80 hectares. My daughter eats truffles and loves cooking them. My son loves being out in the field. And Adele is a great source of commonsense—a handbrake on my wilder ideas.

A truffle is basically an underground mushroom. It starts with an acorn which you germinate and then 'inoculate' the young tree with fungi before planting in specially modified soil. This grows for three to five years, and if all goes according to plan it should produce truffles. We started with hazelnut trees—20,000 of them—but they weren't productive. We've now planted oak trees and as each year passes, the root area gets bigger and more truffles come on.

Over time we've used Lagottas, springer spaniels, English spaniels, Labradors, and kelpies to sniff out the truffles. We currently have five dogs which I've trained and the kelpies are the cleverest. Those dogs can make or break the whole operation. You also need to judge when the truffles are right to be lifted—if you find one today it might have 'catty' notes and so needs few more days before the sweet aroma tells you it is good for lifting.

I've been to France several times to learn more about the industry but the real way you learn all these things is through experience. I like learning from mistakes. In this field there is a lot you can read but 99 per cent of what is written is by scientists with access to small samples, say ten trees in a back paddock. They don't tell you how to control kangaroos or potoroos or discuss the different sorts of microbes.

French truffle expert Pierre-Jean Pebeyre says ours are as good as the best French truffles he's tasted. We're exporting to the USA, Asia and Europe but I'm parochially Tasmanian. We have a wonderful environment, the cleanest air, four definite seasons and a Mediterranean climate so it's easy to market our truffles differently. And quality is our emphasis.

My key transferable skills relate to what happens underground. Having your head in the dirt for 30 years means you learn how soil and water work. Making a lot of money was our original intention but ten years down the track it hasn't happened. I know I'm locked in for the rest of my life. That's okay, every day is different and every day is a challenge and I simply love it.

Tim Terry is Managing Director of Truffles Australis
<www.trufflesaustralis.com.au>

To buy, join or create?

There are a handful of key reasons for wanting to strike out on your own. These might include:

- independence
- flexibility in working hours
- greater freedom
- need to care for family
- a desire to 'prove' yourself
- work–life balance
- increased financial independence

These reasons are important to bear in mind when you encounter the first critical decision you need to make—whether to buy an existing business, join a franchise, or create your own from scratch. Inherent in many of the above-listed reasons is a desire for a better mix of work and home life. And this is when you need to be brutally honest with yourself about the number of hours per week you are able and prepared to commit to a new business. According to ABS statistics, more than a third of small business owners work longer hours (more than 49 per week) compared with just 12 per cent of full-time employees putting in the same hours. Now is the time to decide if this full-on commitment is realistic or if a balanced lifestyle is more likely to be achieved by purchasing a business with a track record rather than heading into the great unknown.

Off the shelf: buying an existing business

There are many reasons why people buy an existing business. One frequently stated reason is that it is safer than starting one up. Statistics on comparable success rates are difficult to uncover and business exits (for a variety of reasons other than financial) are often counted as failures. Even if purchasing an existing business is slightly 'safer', unless you are extremely diligent in assessing the financial statements, you may pay too much for something you could have created for a much lower sum. Factors to consider when buying an existing business include:

- reasons the vendor is selling
- profits for every year of trading
- all costs
- liabilities including warranties, customer rewards and pre-purchase
- sales history, trends and forecasts
- customer database
- technology and internet issues
- tax and legal implications
- staff agreements and remuneration

The above is not an exhaustive list. If you are putting your hard-earned savings on the line it is imperative that you use a reliable accountant and lawyer, preferably those who are experienced in the industry sector of interest. As with all other major transactions, it's *caveat emptor* (buyer beware), once, twice and thrice. The most useful gambit of all, if you are genuinely interested in buying someone else's business, is to take a month's leave and ask if you can work in it to see if it has a good fit with your requirements. Those vendors running a profitable and efficient business should have no problem with this idea. And the others? That's for you to contemplate . . .

Franchising

If buying an established business seems safe, then purchasing a business within a franchise network may seem rock-solid. In Australia franchising is a $130 billion industry employing nearly half a million workers. The term franchise refers to a business system where the owner grants the franchisee the right to operate a replicated business using the same trade name, and documented systems, in return for a purchase price, ongoing fees and a willingness to comply with the stated procedures.

Out of 1.9 million small businesses in Australia today, approximately 3.7 per cent are franchises, or 71,400 units operating in business format franchise units employing a total of 413,500 persons, the majority casual (39 per cent) or permanent part time (23.3 per cent). The pros and cons of owning and managing a franchise are listed in Table 9.1. For those seeking security in their first business venture, the perceived higher rate of success can be a compelling argument. Franchises are also popular for the immediate entry into a network of same-industry professionals selling an identical product or service and guaranteed to be facing similar challenges on a daily basis.

Codes of conduct

But before deciding upon any franchised business, it is imperative that you read the Franchising Code of Conduct. It is easily downloadable

Table 9.1 Buying a franchise	
Sounds good	**Need to think about**
Benefit of larger business network	Possibly restrictive with need to adhere to franchisor conditions
Access to business know-how	Ongoing commitment to pay royalties and advertising fees
Support, particularly in early decision making	Requirements for upgrades
Established product or service	Vulnerability to rogue franchisee behaviour
Stronger bargaining power/group negotiations	Lack of ability for creativity and self-expression
Consistency of product or service	Better suited to team players

Adapted from ACCC *Franchise Manual and Guide to Franchising Code of Conduct*

from the Franchise Council of Australia (FCA) website, listed in the Notes and Resources section, but as it is a 55-page trade practices document, it is hardly bedtime reading. Happily a *Guide to the Franchising Code of Conduct*, published by the Australian Competition and Consumer Commission (ACCC), offers a two-page overview of the things you need to know about the purchase of a franchise. The ACCC also offers a 38-page franchisee manual which covers the essential elements associated with buying a franchise, including a useful FAQs section. Some of the issues discussed include understanding compliance with the Franchising Code of Conduct, knowing your obligations, knowing the information you should be shown, and resolving disputes, should they arise. You also need to be very aware of the fees involved, including an original purchase fee, franchise renewal fees, royalties or commissions and other fees including staff training and advertising.

But do you love it?
How do you evaluate whether a franchise will be right for you? Start with your empathy with the product or service. Do you love it? Do you believe in it? Or is purchasing the right to this brand and business system just a way to make a fast buck? And if it is, how many

hours are you prepared to devote to, say, scooping ice-cream late at night before you want to scream? Speak to existing and previous franchisees—how do they like the brand, the management, the rules of the turf?

Do you know the territory where you will work? You may think you know a local shopping precinct well—but *do you*? Driving by on your way to and from work is not the same as visiting a city or town in the middle of the day, and observing the type of clientele wandering past your (soon-to-be) premises. Do yourself a favour and stalk the business you are planning to buy for a week or two—in rain, hail and shine, early, late and lunchtime. It's worth risking arrest! You may be surprised by your observations. And don't forget the power of an industry organisation. The Franchise Council of Australia has a wealth of information for new chums.

Fast food franchisee:
Hugh Evans

After taking a package following nearly 30 years of teaching, I was sitting reading the newspaper one winter's day and I saw an advert for McDonald's franchisees in Adelaide and Perth. Normally managers become owners but at this time the McDonald's management thought the company needed new blood—people with life experience. I was 49 so I had plenty of that!

Three of us were selected, then followed nine months of interviewing before I was told, 'Congratulations you are a registered applicant—but will need to train for nine months without pay.' I was absolutely over the moon. The training program was fantastic but I struggled. Often I couldn't get the money to balance and you can't go home until you do. I had no business experience—I didn't really know what a bottom line was, but I learnt how to manage a business and refine my people skills. And managing 80 kids and sixteen managers made great use of my previous high-school teaching experience.

Finally our store was ready and my wife, Lizzie, and I moved to Adelaide as owners. We were there ten years and initially lost an enormous amount of borrowed money. I had cashed in my super and spent my redundancy package, thinking we would do very well. I had done the research and homework. Because it was a franchise with resources and support I believed it couldn't fail.

But before long we had lost everything we put into it. I decided to borrow even more. We ran a huge marketing program to sell cheeseburgers at half price for six months. The customers also became more comfortable with me and Lizzie; they loved talking to mature people. We were doing twelve-hour days but we loved it.

Eventually the business turned around, people had a good experience, and it went from nothing to a cash cow. A few years later we got an offer we couldn't refuse and moved to the beach.

Hugh Evans now paints and runs Hugh Gallery in Flinders, Victoria <www.hughgallery.com>

Creating a startup

Watch out, world! For years you've lived and breathed the dream of creating your own startup business. Your concept is brilliant; no one else has even got close to something this clever. Your determination is second only to your passion. You're hot to trot. And nothing is going to stand in your way!

Your chances of success

At a simple level success means staying in business. Forests have been chopped down to publish the thousands of books advising potential entrepreneurs on the qualities they will need to be guaranteed of business success. But what exactly *is* business success? As previously discussed, in *Free Agent Nation*, Dan Pink suggests that many small business owners are starting to free themselves of 'old business' success measures—heavily centred on profit and prestige—and starting to see success in a more personal way. This includes 'wins' such as the ability to have frequent family holidays, time to care for an ailing parent or the opportunity to mix business travel with personal time out. It could even mean the opportunity to work on projects with stimulating colleagues and low (or even no) remuneration but loads of work satisfaction in the form of personal development. This 'success' might also deliver a mix of working hours and free time that was simply unavailable when you were a wage slave.

It's your startup, so it's up to you to define what your business success will look and feel like. Find out your preferred weighting of these factors in Table 9.2. Give each factor a rating out of ten, then give them a ranking of most important to least important in the right-hand column.

Table 9.2 Your business success		
Will you measure your success by:	**Rating /10**	**Ranking of this factor**
Working hours per week		
Working environment		
Work–life balance		
Peer interaction		
Lack of or number of employees		
Time out for pre-determined rewards or obligations		
Remuneration		
Decision-making roles		
Family involvement		
Travel requirements or opportunities		

This weighting should start to reveal the shape of the business you think will suit you best. And it's important to share these results with those who live under the same roof, to allow any potential erroneous assumptions to be dealt with.

Reducing your risk factors

Businesses most commonly fail because the principals are lacking in one or more of the five essential 'P's; qualities that no budding business owner can afford to ignore:

- personality   [score   /20]
- passion   [score   /20]
- persistence   [score   /20]
- plan   [score   /20]
- pockets   [score   /20]

A quick appraisal of each of these aspects—as described in the following paragraphs—should enable you to award yourself a score out of 20 per quality in the brackets above. Your score should total at least 80 out of the possible 100. Why? Because, if you are typical of the majority of small business owners, you will devote most of your waking hours to this project, probably for many years. You need to have the attributes and assets to support your idea. And hopefully you will score well in each of the categories, and not highly in four with a big fat zero in one. It's tough but true. Successful business people are usually all-rounders when it comes to skills, cash management and fortitude.

Personality

We have seen a plethora of 'reality' TV shows in recent years which basically tell us that a leopard can change its spots—it just needs some help in the form of an executive coach, or dancing teacher, or a jab or two of Botox—whatever it takes. In business, as in real life, a leopard rarely changes its spots. If your personality is the shy retiring type and you like to work in a large organisation performing specialised tasks for a set number of hours per week it is highly likely you will find the topsy turvy world that owner/managers continually face to be entirely confronting—and very uncomfortable.

You can probably massage or enhance skills you don't currently possess, but will need, to achieve your goals. But your basic personality is something that is fairly set. If you're into the steady and predictable, running your own business may be entirely too stressful a venture.

Proving passion

As with personality, passion is something you just can't manufacture. If you have an abiding passion for your new business idea—a true itch that won't go away—and you have been faithful to this idea for an extended period of time, award yourself a high score. If, however, in your mind, the jury is well and truly out, you may not possess the amount of passion needed to weather the commitment to making your new project work.

Persistence

Persistence or determination is what is going to take your business through tough times. No honest business operator will pretend that the early days are easy. They may be exciting, challenging or frenetic—but these words are usually euphemisms for BHW—bloody hard work. Knockbacks are a common feature of business startups and many captains of industry will talk about persisting ten, twenty or even thirty times with one tough client—only to find this hard-won sale is the turning point in the success of their venture. Do *you* have this sort of persistence?

The plan

No matter whether you are planning a business to rival that of Google, or hoping to supplement your income with some extra dollars trading on eBay, there is simply no avoiding the need to do a thorough business plan. Business plans are not the accounting nightmare you fear. They are much more user-friendly than that. They are documents which 'walk' you through the essentials of your idea. The key elements in an effective business plan are well explained on the not-for-profit Business Enterprise Centres (BEC) website. (See the Notes and Resources section.)

(Deep) pockets

Startup capital is one of the most under-estimated aspects of new businesses. The only thing that will allow you to start a business with too little capital and get away with it is an uncanny ability to project and manage cash flow. Whilst walking the cash-flow tightrope may be viewed by optimists as exhilarating, it's also an exhausting waste of time which could be better spent on basics such as marketing and managing; tasks that could be increasing your revenue, in other words. So now is a good time to address the critical issue of cash. Do you want to delay your business plans until you have saved or secured sufficient capital, ensuring reserves for a rainy day? Or do you wish to create a rock-solid cash-flow projection which proves you can weather the metaphorical business storms? Again, the BEC website is a good source of user-friendly information on cash-flow management.

Government support

Many entrepreneurs do the hard yards by themselves as they are unaware of the extensive resources and support that federal, state and territory and local governments offer to new businesses, from conception to establishment and beyond. Described as the Australian Government's principal business resource, the <business.gov.au> website offers a wealth of material to those considering a new venture. This information includes a 35-page downloadable PDF entitled *Starting Your Business* that comprehensively covers the basic information and which really should be required reading before any individual is granted an ABN.

> *Establishing a new business can create an enormous strain on your finances, your family, your social life and your emotions. Your will have to work long hours . . . your income may become uncertain . . . it could fluctuate enormously as a result of factors you cannot control. You will face the unrelenting*

pressure of having to make decisions and solve problems when you are not sure about what to do.

—John English and Babette Moate, Discovering New Business Opportunities

Chapter wrap

Take heart. The statistics of the ABS offer the surprising confirmation that small business owners are at least as secure as full-time employees—if not more so. If you have a burning ambition to stamp your mark on a new business venture there's very little reason why you shouldn't succeed.

If, that is, you are prepared to do the extensive homework and preparation beforehand. This chapter refers to just a few of the many forms of support available to help you with your planning

So don't just sit there, go for it!

Connecting the career dots

Natasha Boyd and Tim Terry have created two very different types of business enterprise. Both, however, were prepared to put in the time and effort to research their propositions and to take on new skills.

Natasha's 'by the book' career segue demonstrates a major change achieved by a series of small steps. Her move into a different organisation and work arrangement (self-employed) as well as sector (retail) also involved a change of location from country to city. First Natasha completed a course on running a bookshop, then trained to use the required software, joined an independent bookseller association and used her teaching experience in childhood literacy to create a niche bookshop.

Tim used his extensive knowledge of soils and drainage to extend his farming operations to include truffles. He remains in the same industry, but with such a different product he has needed to research and learn on the job in the attempt to deliver quality produce on a consistent basis.

Despite extensive research and training and the fact he bought into a 'safer' form of business investment, a high-profile franchise, Hugh Evans initially lost his savings. It was only by borrowing money and using his creative marketing skills that he managed to keep the business afloat.

10

New tricks

Old stereotypes die hard. And none moreso than the cliché of the old fogey worker—a bald-headed cardie-clad grumpy old man hopeless at technology and new systems, desperately clinging to the job he's held for decades. In the past, older workers were the first to go during a credit squeeze. But many organisations have learnt that the depth of knowledge and hard-won experience mature workers possess can be difficult, if not impossible, to replace. Now that the 'dream' of full-time retirement has been revealed as a myth, many workers are planning on working into their sixties, seventies and beyond. This chapter looks at the employment prospects for mature workers, the reasons they will enjoy longer, more productive working lives and how they can ensure that they remain workplace-relevant. Whether it's a search for significance or a desire to top up the super—or both—the new workplace offers a much friendlier environment for the resilient. New legislation protecting the rights of older workers will reinforce this change but older workers will also have to play their part by ensuring their skills are up-to-date and accepting the demise of the notion of a 'job for life'. The end result is a much more exciting, multigenerational work scene.

> *To do nothing is no longer an option.*
> **—Charles Handy, The Empty Raincoat**

Old dogs

In 2003 the BBC created a television show with a winning formula. It was originally aired as a one-off, but when it drew 67 million viewers, the Beeb decided a series was definitely the way to go. Titled *New Tricks,* it starred a rogue's gallery of older detectives brought out of retirement to solve cold cases. Despite the name of the show, these 'old dogs' employed few 'new tricks' depending instead on time-honoured policing methods to get their man.

At one level this program subverted the ageist workplace stereotype of older workers who are 'past it' being overtaken by bright young things with higher qualifications. But at another level, it reinforced the notion that using traditional policing was the most effective way to get results, particularly if this involved eschewing training or the use of new technologies.

That's with the exception of the nerdy member of the team, Brian, played by Alun Armstrong. An interesting character with a quirky mathematical brain, Brian lives on the internet and makes connections few others can see.

Brian is, in fact, the only one of the old dogs who really employs the 'new tricks' of the trade as a way of remaining workplace-relevant.

The stereotype

Sadly, Brian is an example rarely seen or acknowledged when the conversation turns to older workers, retirement and pension funding.

Instead the discussion is usually so negative it is enough to send a relatively 'normal' 50-year-old bolting to the gym or beautician in order to tone up, with or without the aid of Botox or implants, in case their age (a fact of life) is held against them in the quest to stay employed and employable.

How it came to this is a long, long story, but a brief look at the history of retirement is instructive.

In *Prime Time,* an overview of the ways in which the talents of older Americans might be recognised and utilised, author Marc Freedman looks back upon the construction of Sun City, the first purpose-built retirement village, in Phoenix, Arizona, as a turning point in the way Americans were encouraged to view—in fact, to anticipate—their retirement. The marketers, Del Webb, had seen the potential of a longer living, slightly wealthier segment of the population who would embrace the opportunity to live a life free of responsibilities but full of golf. Some 12 per cent of Americans aged over 65 now live in retirement cities or complexes, so this concept has obviously struck gold for many companies.

In Australia the number of retirement village residents aged over 65 is just 5 per cent, so we have been far less eager to embrace the all play, no work promise. In fact, the balance of 95 per cent of men and women aged over 65 who are eschewing a retirement village lifestyle presents a robust rebuttal of the life of leisure.

The interest, however, lies not in the 7 per cent difference between Australia and the US in the uptake of this way of retirement village living. It is in how and why we ever allowed ourselves to be told that our final 20, 30 or more years on earth should be spent in some sort of adult kindergarten. When did the concept of not working as you got older take such a grip on the popular imagination?

Tim Lane:
A step into a tougher world

profile

I failed science at university where I basically spent three years floundering, then spent sixteen months working in an Edgell pea cannery in northern Tasmania.

One long weekend in March, 1972, when all my mates were back at university, I was drinking, smoking and playing pool in the local pub. I remember a boozy conversation about football and horse racing with a local radio commentator, Elton Alexander, from station 7AD in Devonport. He asked if I would like to go along and see how calling worked. I woke up the next day with a hangover and thought, My

God, did I have that conversation? I'd already applied for a sports journalism role at Channel Nine Launceston and been knocked back. But I thought if I followed up, Elton might not remember me or might be embarrassed.

Four or five weeks later he walked into the same pub—we were both on our first beer—and he mentioned he was disappointed I hadn't followed up his offer. I said I would be there next Saturday which was 6 May 1972, the local football derby. I sat there while he called the first quarter. Then I joined him in the second quarter. The station only paid him $20 a week, so he couldn't pay me but he gave me some cash at the end of the season.

Shortly afterwards I picked up a part-time job with the ABC in Launceston with the prospect of a full-time position in the sports department which I gained after eighteen months. I then gained my dream job in the sports department of the ABC in Melbourne some five years later.

[In 2003 Tim left the ABC after 30 years of broadcasting, including Australian Rules football, international cricket, five Olympic Games and five Commonwealth Games. He left because, after years of single parenting, he had found someone with whom he wanted to spend his time, and his gruelling travel commitments were impossible to reconcile with his commitment to his new partner.]

It was a personal decision to step down and not easily done. I had a very comfortable position at the ABC—I was then the main man in the footy season and a member of the international cricket broadcasting team. This involved a component of power; you owned the territory and felt relevant in a prominent and respected role. There was a moment during my transitional phase when I felt a sense of relevance deprivation syndrome.

In a way the move from full-time work with the ABC has helped prepare me for an eventual retirement transition. I haven't pondered too deeply about retirement, but I guess some sort of wind-down is inevitable. The world sees us differently as we grow older. Things do change, whether we like it or not. I am conscious of the need to convey that I still have energy and enthusiasm. I hope my retirement is a fair way off, but I have entered a transitional phase. When I was on the staff of the ABC my work was one-dimensional, as it was in radio, covering different sports in different seasons. Now I am a freelance broadcaster on TV, and radio, and a newspaper writer. With the precarious nature of football televising rights, it is possible one or more of these jobs could go. I always need to bear that in mind.

So if one role goes, perhaps the other two will still be there. I also do some public speaking and am about to start writing a book, so I'm employed for the foreseeable future. Maintaining a sense of fulfilment and relevance still matters. I'm not sure if people get better with age but in my sort of work you get better at some things. You gain experience, knowledge about a topic, self-knowledge, and a broader context. You know more about the history of a sport—there's a lot that's stored away.

Personally I like hearing older voices, people who've been around a long time. The flipside is youthful ambition—young people have unsatisfied, unrequited hunger for achievement—and you can feel that ambition. It's not entirely competitive. But there are only so many jobs to go around in the commentary box and the jobs are the prize for the best.

Elements of the game of football have changed significantly and I refer to these changes regularly. (I suspect) my younger colleagues would just like me to get over it! Identifying myself as an older observer of the game can also make me vulnerable—put a target on my back again. My move from radio to TV meant I was going to the most conspicuous area of media performance. TV commentators can be judged pretty harshly. You're talking over pictures so you're in danger of being a distraction. It was a step from a cosy position where I had been more than fairly treated by audience and media reviewers into a far tougher world. It's my seventh season on TV and I think I'm getting better.

As with all public performance, commentating isn't without its difficulties. People who do it well make it look easy. It's often said that public speaking is one of the most frightening experiences you can face, so it's not done without a certain amount of wear and tear. I feel as though I've had extraordinary good fortune to have the opportunity to do the work I do. But one day I'll say that's it and will feel a huge sense of relief.

Tim Lane is a radio broadcaster, television commentator and writer

The numbers look good

The concept of retirement is really one that has only had currency in the last 60 years and it is fast becoming obsolete.

There is a reason people didn't retire in earlier centuries. We simply didn't live long enough. In 1800 the average life expectancy for an Australian man was 38 years. In 1900 this had increased to 55 years, so generally speaking, people were still too young (i.e. productive) to retire. Today it's 78.7 for males and 83.5 for females. But people now say they *feel* too young to retire. With active bodies and minds and a lot of fun yet to be had, they don't necessarily only want to work full time, but are happy to consider a mix of full- and part-time work. Recent research from the University of Tasmania, the Australian Survey of Retirement Attitudes and Motivations (ASRAM), confirms 62 per cent of Baby Boomers are seeking a phased and meaningful transition to retirement with regular part-time work, with 75 per cent wishing to do so in their present occupation. A significant 82 per cent desire to pass on their knowledge through mentoring.

Phil Ruthven
The need to 'get it'

From a market perspective the challenge has always been to get enough workers to keep everybody alive. The optimum number is 4/10 citizens working full time or a combination of full- and part-time workers. This ratio has not changed for centuries across most countries. One hundred years ago, at Federation, we were struggling to get 4 workers per 10. So 4 per cent of the workforce, aged under fourteen, was needed to keep society 'alive'. There was no retirement; workers were needed and people died too young. Long term the situation for older workers is good. Our economy will need workers. It's rarely acknowledged in the media, the reporters are all too young. Because they have no sense of history or perspective they just don't get it.

The long view

Having a long view of history, as Phil Ruthven notes, helps a lot.

The current 'golden years' perception of retirement is both recent and wrong.

There has been a raft of vested interests involved in selling the idea of a retirement 'stage'. These vested interests have a lot of money at stake. They include organisations such as financial services, property developers, drug companies, health and beauty marketers, travel purveyors and more.

But while the development and promulgation of the golden age is helpful to the bottom line of retirement village operators and other companies marketing products to ageing citizens of the western world, it is extremely detrimental to those who wish to enjoy long and productive lives. These industries that portray older people as only fit to be put out to pasture have raised generational barriers where none previously existed.

A tale of two Americans

It's not clear if George Burns and Ernest Hemingway ever met. And, ostensibly, they have nothing in common except their country of birth. Burns was short, funny and lived a long life, with one wife. Hemingway was tall, brooding, had four wives, and took his own life just after turning 61. But on one point they were aligned. Burns, who was born in 1896 and lived until he was 100, said: 'Age to me means nothing. I can't get old; I'm working. I was old when I was twenty-one and out of work. As long as you're working, you stay young. When I'm in front of an audience, all that love and vitality sweeps over me and I forget my age.'

True to his style, Hemingway, born three years later in 1899, was much more succinct: 'Retirement is the ugliest word in the language.'

The retirement aberration

The concept of retirement, or a third age of leisure-laden golden years, may indeed be false, but the ageing of the global population is very real.

Population histograms were traditionally referred to as pyramids owing to the shape created by a larger percentage of people aged less than 50. Such charts are now more likely to resemble cubes, as the shape of generations changes with, for the first time in the history of the planet, more people aged over 60 than under fifteen expected to occur in 2050. This is due to many factors, but mainly because of the confluence of three main demographic trends:

- Longevity is increasing. In 1900 an Australian male was expected to live to 55, a female to 59. Current life expectancy is 78.7 and 83.5 respectively. An astonishing 24 years has been added to the average expected lifespan of the average male.

- The outlook for quality of life during these extra years is also very positive. At 60, Australian men's bodies are no longer broken by years of toil in a mine or on a railroad, nor women's bodies worn out by bearing and raising eight, nine or ten children.
- At the same time, the fertility rate has fallen dramatically, largely due to the contraceptive pill and a weakening of previously strong religious observance.

The result of these three trends is fewer younger people, more older. Fewer younger workers to contribute to the national tax base, more older workers likely to be hired. As seen in Chapter 2, technological changes have, and will continue to, transform the way we work. The 'man' is no longer required to perform *man*ual jobs, with equipment and computers increasingly available to perform repetitive tasks. Work may be demanding and stressful but the 'hard labour' component is waning in most developed nations.

According to <www.aboutseniors.com.au>, the workplace experience of older workers is chequered, to say the least. In research conducted in June 2009, 33 per cent of respondents, who were aged between 50 and 75, reported experiencing problems of age discrimination, and 29 per cent stated they would work more hours per week if suitable work was available. For half the respondents, retirement did not mean stopping full-time work, with many commenting that the retirement years should provide an opportunity to get off the career ladder and take a job you really enjoy.

Good news, bad news

As with most major societal upheavals, the ageing of our population can be seen as a positive or a negative. To date, most media portrayals of the increase in the proportion of older people have been very negative. Older people are normally portrayed as 'past it', with little to offer and rapidly declining skills and powers. They are shown to be entering the 'deficit' phase of life, a drain on the public purse, their years of experience and hard-won wisdom of seemingly little value to other ages. But as more and more gerontological research is undertaken and published, the deficit view is being challenged—and rejected. As Stanley Miller, President of the International Association of Universities of the Third Age declares, 'This deficit model of old age is out-dated, with a large and growing body of evidence leading to a much more positive view . . . where attributes and activities determine the appropriate classification rather than simple chronology.' Miller's observation emphasises the critical point all older workers, and those who would benefit from their talents, must learn. No longer should age be a determining factor when it comes to someone's suitability for employment. It is their attributes and attitudes which should count them in or out.

No longer should age be a determining factor when it comes to someone's suitability for employment.

The noise associated with the recent global financial downturn has tended to mask another piece of good news for older workers; that the structural skills shortage in developed nations has not disappeared. Short term we may experience an increase in redundancies and unemployment. Longer term—three, four or more years down the track—the western world will experience a very strong need for experienced workers in the tertiary, quaternary and quinary sectors of the economy. And those older workers who have stayed abreast of new developments and new technologies will be able to negotiate new roles which will be more on their terms than those of an employer.

Time for self-actualisation

In 1954, psychologist Abraham Maslow described a hierarchy of needs. The most basic needs—food, clothing, shelter—were at the bottom of the list, whilst security, social needs and the psychological wants for self-esteem and recognition ranked more highly. The highest level of need, according to Maslow, is the need for self-actualisation; the need to fulfil one's self, to grow, to be the best one can. The

Leonard Cohen:
Topping up the super

There is no end to the pleasure and value an older worker can bring. Consider Leonard Cohen who, with his band, hit the road to perform more than 80 concerts during 2008-9. Cohen discovered his retirement savings had vanished when his financial adviser mismanaged his assets. But this 73-year-old proved his assets extended far beyond the financial, filling stadiums from Belfast to New York and all over Australia, winning crowd adulation and 'best of' awards as he made his way around the globe.

Leonard Cohen is a poet and singer-songwriter

consistent message from research about older workers' motivations is that the desire to achieve worldly success, particularly of a financial or professional nature, is likely to give way to a stronger need to make one's mark doing something that will create a valuable legacy.

This sense of legacy forms part of the concept of 'generativity' noted by Professor George Valliant in his book *Ageing Well*. Valliant defines the quality of generativity as 'the giving of oneself and taking care of the next generation in a way that outlives the self'. It's not surprising then, that as we age, we start to contemplate our achievements thus far and to wonder about the impact we have made. This contemplation obviously includes thoughts about what we have passed on to our children, but it can also focus very much on our body of work. What have we created? How have we added value? Will there be a eulogy on the good we have added to humankind?

Funeral notes

It's become a bit of a cliché for career counsellors and life coaches to ask people to imagine their funeral and what their nearest and dearest might say as a way of understanding the things that matter most—and the things we truly wish to attempt. But clichés are clichés for a good reason. They come from enduring truths. The need to believe we have, or will, make a real difference is extremely important to most human beings. As our work lives evolve from the early years when it seems the world is our oyster, to a time when our options and opportunities seem to be narrowing, we start to adopt ways of working which better reflect the self we have come to know, rather than the self we believe the world expects us to be.

At one level this might mean a time of disappointment, a time of acknowledging our inability to achieve things that mattered and a time when our failures seem more abundant than our successes. But the recognition of not achieving a goal is often the first step to freeing up our vision to set new and different goals which can be simultaneously more achievable and extremely satisfying.

The transitions in life's second half offer a special kind of opportunity to break with the social conditioning that has carried us successfully this far and to do something really new and different. It is a season more in tune than the earlier ones with the deeper promptings of the spirit.

—William Bridges, *Transitions*

William Bridges uses the Hindu notion of four seasons of life to explain our third age as that of the forest dweller; someone who, having completed their time as a householder (worker, family member and provider) now reaches a stage where they will retreat to reflect and to enjoy a time of inner search and discovery. It is often more commonly understood in western society (for those who are parents) as the 'empty nesters' phase when adult children take responsibility for their own futures and their parents can start to treat their own needs as a priority. Whatever name we give to this stage, when considered from the perspective of our working lives, it represents a move away from the need for material rewards and status and towards a need for employment that makes a difference. The old myth of retirement would have us understand this is a graceful and relieved departure from the workplace, a withdrawal. In fact it is the opposite. It is the renouncing of the need to work for dollars alone. It is a move toward much more meaningful employment.

The search for significance

The search for significant or more satisfying work is a highly individual and personal pursuit. It is not for others to frame the terms of reference of your sense of purpose and meaning. Your significant work may just as easily be creative, or nurturing or political or community-based. The important thing is to feel a connection to something far larger than yourself. Often a short stint of voluntary work can offer experience of a different kind and build your confidence in your own skills, whilst adding value to the lives of others. Consider the example of Kathryn Wasserman Davis who, on her hundredth birthday in 2007, created a charity named Project for Peace which gives $1 million (i.e. $10,000 x 100 grants) each year to young people who submit projects to further world peace. Most of us would believe we had 'run our race' by this age and were of little further value, but this extraordinary woman saw a need to help young people help others—and filled it. Nice one!

Elizabeth Broderick
Resilience through learning

In Australia, the *Age Discrimination Act* is widely recognised as one of the weakest of all the discrimination acts. For example, it doesn't provide for a dedicated commissioner, unlike the *Sex Discrimination Act* or the *Race Discrimination Act*. Despite a number of age discrimination actions being commenced in the Federal Court, not one has been successful at the federal level. And yet we hear of cases such as the retail organisation which required applicants for the role of shop assistant to do squats in the interview. With large groups of older people who need to work there is evidence they will fall into social decline and poverty if they can't get work because of their age. For such people, the bar of age discrimination sits above any concern about their skills, education and experience. If employers decide that because of your age certain qualities will automatically apply, then we all suffer.

Mature-age workers are no different to any other age group; some are energetic and some are not. There are, however, some positive attributes associated with older workers which employers often mention. These include their depth of experience, understanding of broader life context, confidence in sharing ideas and reliability. They've also seen cycles of change—the good times and the bad times—and so are comfortable, when things are down, that they will come back.

There's a lot of debate about the best training for older workers, but I'm in no doubt a key strategy is to build resilience into our working lives and that this is best done by taking a lifelong approach to learning, whether formal, on the job or informal. We also need to stay connected with those who may have opportunities for future work rather than starting a flurry of activity when building our careers and very little at other times.

Elizabeth Broderick is the Sex Discrimination Commissioner and Commissioner responsible for Age Discrimination <www.hreoc.gov.au>

Your workplace rights

Although it may not feel like it—should you be the sole applicant aged over 50 in the office of a junior headhunter, sweating over your chances of being hired—there have been major advances in the past few years when it comes to the rights of older workers.

There is no statutory retirement age in Australia. The Age Pension is currently offered to males at age 65 and females aged 55 to 63, depending upon birth year (although this will increase to 67 by 2023). Currently many Australians are retiring at relatively youthful ages—a recent ABS survey states that 76 per cent of men had retired before 63 and 76 per cent of women had retired before the age of 60. The growing recognition of the coming skills shortage has seen many new government initiatives to encourage workers to stay in the workplace. These are an interesting mix of the carrot and the stick. The carrot includes the Pension Bonus Scheme, introduced by the Howard Government in 1998 and effectively closed to new entrants by the Rudd Government in the May 2009 Budget, but still offering cash incentives for those already registered who are working later and thus delaying their access to an Age Pension.

Another important piece of legislation of direct benefit to older workers was quietly introduced late in 2008. This relates to the *Age Discrimination Act, ACT 2004* and effectively widens the Act by the removal of the 'dominant reason' test. This means that a person need only show that their age was *one* of the reasons they were discriminated against. This will harmonise the Act with other federal unlawful discrimination laws. It will hopefully also mean that job applicants such as the flight attendant who attended an airline interview will no longer have to sing and dance to prove that they can fit in with a youthful workplace culture.

There are many other safeguards for older workers which cover getting a job, terms and conditions, training, promotion, dismissal and redundancy, although voluntary work and domestic duties in private households are not as well protected. Fairer legislation is a help, but it can't change society's attitudes overnight. It is difficult to redress decades of ageist negativism in the workplace, and so it is helpful for mature workers to arm themselves with some of the following facts, compiled by the Business, Work and Ageing Centre for Research at Swinburne University, before fronting up for an interview or selection process.

Mythbusting

In reality, older workers:

- are just as productive as younger workers
- are not more costly than younger workers
- use experience to offset any decline in cognitive ability
- are quite capable of learning new skills
- perform just as well as younger workers
- are interested in career and self-development
- are often more flexible than younger workers
- contribute to a diversified workplace culture
- do not necessarily want to retire

Flipping the truck

Although most workers are starting to benefit from growing flexibility in many workplaces, another helpful techological change is the robotisation of many functions of manual labour which now means that older manufacturing workers are finding it easier to retain their jobs, with the help of machine 'co-workers'. Two examples: in America one company has looked at the traditional process of truck manufacture. Valued older employees were finding it increasingly difficult to bend down to work underneath the chassis of the trucks being assembled. The solution? A machine which literally flips the truck chassis upside down so workers can now remain upright during the assembly line process. For this innovation the manufacturer, International Trucks, won one of ten international Innovative Employer Awards from the American Association of Retired Persons (AARP) in 2008.

A similar story comes from Singapore, a country where the government of Lee Hsien Loong has seen the age wave coming and has put major reforms in place, creating the Council of the Third Age, to research and present solutions to keep workplaces age-friendly. Older hospital workers who were finding it increasingly difficult to strip and remake beds now benefit from ergonomically designed equipment which protects their physical wellbeing. In fact, in most western nations there are strenuous government efforts to foster more age-friendly workplaces. Why? Because they have seen the forecasts and know the skills shortage is real, despite the recent global financial downturn.

Flexibility rules

The changes in the workplace previously discussed are nothing short of a boon to older workers. Research conducted earlier this year by Ken Dytchwald of Age Wave in the United States confirms that 60 per cent of Baby Boomers see retirement as a time not of leisure or rest (only 20 per cent thought this) but of new purpose, new priorities, new careers and a new opportunity to give back. An opportunity for a new and exciting chapter in life was the description confirmed by 60 per cent of respondents, with 70 per cent saying they wanted work in the mix. This is entirely consistent with the findings of Rutgers University Centre for Work and Living, which reports nearly 70 per cent of respondents thought retirement was an opportunity to seek either full- or part-time work including 15 per cent who wanted to start a new business. Only 13 per cent wanted to stop work completely.

Australian research, such as the previously quoted ASRAM report, also confirms older workers do not consider themselves to have a use-by date. So for those who feel that they still have a lot to give, the stars appear to be aligning. Particularly when we consider the key changes in the way we work—where work is moving from the full-time, five days a week job toward a series of customised assignments which allow for a more individualised approach including negotiation of time and place. With appropriate technology, these work commitments can often be met on-site, off-site, during the day or during the night. This increasing flexibility in the shape and delivery of work suits well the desire of older workers to work fewer hours in a more flexible manner. The fewer/more flexible model also better matches the well-documented desire of older workers to give back, to volunteer, and to spend more time with family and friends.

Connie Vallis:
The last word on computer literacy

This year I celebrated my birthday by doing something special. I didn't paddle a canoe around Sydney Harbour, or climb the Bridge or attempt a parachute jump or anything quite that easy. Instead I accepted a real challenge.

With the need to upgrade my five-year-old computer, I enrolled in a 'Build Your Own Computer Course' at Computer Pals—The Hills, where I am a foundation member and trainer of fundamentals.

Computers are such fun. They occupy a huge part of my life. So with much excitement I went ahead and built my own, finding the whole experience wonderfully rewarding. Under the expert guidance of my tutor, Ken, slowly the mysteries of what makes this marvellous machine perform began to magically unravel. I learnt the real need for a motherboard and all its peripheral input and output devices. And a circuit board too, and a CPU, the absolute brain of all computers. And I'm less ignorant of important terminologies like RAM, hard drives, storage devices, floppy and CD drives.

I soon discovered them to be real objects, patiently waiting for me to install them. Yes . . . me, a 76-year-old mother of four and granny of eleven who had taken the plunge to piece together this technological jigsaw. I remember thinking to myself as I worked, was it just ten years ago that my biggest computer challenge was correctly turning my machine on or off, frequently clicking on the wrong thing and fearful of what to do next? And what about all that confusing jargon such as screen savers, icons, menu bars, fonts, clipboards and taskbars?

Yes ... yes ... it was all so daunting. But not now! Not anymore. Now at last I can believe I am computer literate and able to converse confidently with the so-called experts.

My new PC and I are really compatible. Together we are able to perform many remarkable feats. We create interesting letters, enhance special photos, download beautiful music and speak to and explore the world, from right here in the comfort of my home. So get with it, folks, and buy a computer. Or better still—build your own. It really is so much fun.

If I can do it, so can you.

Connie Vallis is a member and trainer at Computer Pals for Seniors, which is a member of the Australian Seniors Computing Clubs Association (ASCCA), <www.ascca.org.au>

And the catch is?

There are no fairies at the bottom of the garden, nor is there a dream flexi assignment waiting for you to leave full-time work and claim it. Whilst it is becoming much more common to renegotiate a role which involves a five-day week into one including telecommuting or a nine-day fortnight, or similar, the catch is that to revamp your work experience you will need to revamp your thinking about how you will engage with the new world of work. It's all very well to become excited at the notion of being one of a network of specialists collaborating and sharing expertise online. But if you aren't prepared to stay abreast of new technologies this is hardly going to happen.

In fact, the need to stay up-to-date with technology is a much stiffer requirement than just being aware of new software, systems, new toys and their applications. It's just as important to understand *how* the widely adopted technologies can and will change the way people work. From group scheduling on a social networking site, to using Microsoft Messenger or Twitter as a team update tool, to mastering a Global Positioning System (GPS), the nature and priority of our work tasks has shifted, as has our interaction with colleagues. If you don't 'get' that Messenger is the tool the team wishes to use for updates during a three-day conference, you will be out of the loop as well as out of work. If you don't understand how the use of a PDA benefits the kitchen staff you probably won't use it effectively enough to keep your waitressing job. If you're not comfortable searching the internet then work at the local library is probably now beyond your reach.

Get it?

Don't expect deference

Another important understanding of the new world of work is the collapse of rank and hierarchy. Those aged over 50 will recall when they started work that the boss, almost without exception one of the oldest people on staff, was the boss and deserved respect for that fact alone. This usually meant being called Mr, Mrs or Miss (no Ms in those days) and as a new chum you would go out to buy their lunch, or make their tea, perhaps even stand when they entered the room (yes, seriously). When they made a decision you abided by it, without argument.

Well, you've probably noticed things have changed quite a lot. With the reduction of middle management and the rise of flatter management structures, the 'team' in many cases is now the decision maker. And the team will often be led by the most competent member of staff, not necessarily the most senior or oldest. The decision of the team leader will often be challenged, and team members may decide to overrule the leader. It smacks of democracy, and for those used to a more authoritarian, perhaps paternalistic style of leadership, it's definitely unsettling. Get used to it. It's workplace reality and the only way forward in a multigenerational workforce.

Shuttlework

But wait, there's more—the shuttle job. Not only is the nine-to-five workday becoming outmoded, so is the concept of work versus retirement. This aspect was also raised in the Age Wave research, where 43 per cent of respondents saw 'retirement' as the opportunity to go back and forth between periods of work and periods of leisure. So let's give it a name such as 'shuttlework'. It's not full-time work, although when engaged on a project, be it landscaping a garden, or writing a thesis, it could well involve fourteen-hour days. It's not 'retirement'—not when more than half your time is in paid employment contracts. No, it's shuttlework.

Chapter wrap

There's a lot of good news for older workers in the new world of work. If you've kept up your skills and personal development you'll be wanted, in fact fought over, in the marketplace. This demand means skilled workers can embrace the flexibility they have longed for and create a work brief that includes flexible hours, location and style of work. Their work assignments will be custom-made.

The old concept of retirement as a time devoted solely to leisure has been irrelevant for a while, but it can now be officially ditched as a label for the last few decades of our lives. As a society we will know that we have matured, along with our workers, when we remove the 'R' word from our lexicon and stop thinking in terms of withdrawal for active and able 50, 60 and 70-year-olds. When we allow, if not encourage, all ages and stages to move from work to rest and back again without fear of prejudice or penalty. And when age is no longer required to be listed on a résumé.

That's when we'll know we've really made it.

Connecting the career dots

Tim Lane made a transition from full-time employment with one organisation, the ABC, for personal reasons. This resulted in a multi-faceted freelance career, still in sport, but as a contractor for more than three media companies, combining television, print and radio as well as public speaking. He sees it as a positive transition, given the uncertain nature of football broadcasting rights.

Connie Vallis took on a technological challenge far beyond the capabilities of most people, regardless of age. With the assistance of her local computer club she learnt how to build her own PC. She hasn't just kept up with technology, she's ahead of it. Go Connie!

11
Your time starts now

There's lots of freedom. You are your own boss, you can build a strong relationship with the passengers—you are really running your own small business. This is bus driving—there are beautiful people out there and I love it.

—Lisa Shergold, gospel-singing bus driver

In Chapter 1 we considered two scenarios. The first where you would leap out of bed eager to embrace the new day and the work you do. The second where you feel irretrievably stuck in the wrong career, perhaps the wrong life.

Now you've had the opportunity to consider your own work history and your current role and whether this role offers the sense of fulfilment described in the opening chapter. How does it match up to what you think really satisfying work looks and feels like?

Let's revisit Hugh Mackay's thoughts summarised into four key points, on why work matters:

- the sense of *connection* we have when working in a stimulating setting with a like-minded tribe
- the sense of *gratification* we receive upon the completion of satisfying tasks

- the opportunity to feel of *value*—often measured by the payment we receive
- the sense of *relevance* work can deliver—a 'potent symbol that we are not finished'

These four benefits of meaningful work are echoed by the people profiled in this book when they summarise the value that their new career directions have delivered.

Underlying these comments is also a sense of excitement about their future, the challenges that will come.

In theory *What Next?* can help everyone rethink their career paths and move towards a more satisfying work experience.

But in practice it won't.

It can only provide strategies and ideas to those who are ready, willing and able to open their minds to new ways of thinking about work and prepared to let go of preconceived notions of who they are and what they've done up to now.

Let's summarise the key learnings from the previous ten chapters before looking at the ten critical steps you will need to embrace if you are to remain not only employment-relevant, but also productively engaged in work which excites you.

First we considered the rapid pace of change in the way we do our work. Much of this change is driven not only by new technologies, but also by the makeup of the workforce—now more diverse than ever before—with more women, more older workers, and an improved understanding of how much workplaces can gain from ethnic, cultural and multigenerational diversity.

Another continuing thread is choice—our ability to make work choices, the way choices we have made, and have yet to make, will continue to shape our future careers. We've looked at the factors behind our choices and whether these are based on internal needs or connected with external measures such as education, skills and experience. The number of jobs and specialisations continues to increase while older ways of working are disappearing. This choice can confuse, so some strategies for career shopping and making good decisions have been discussed. In particular the Connect your career dots grid has introduced the concept of career change by sector, role, organisation, work arrangement, location or learning. This way of understanding the different aspects of work change allows you to plan incremental or radical change as and when it suits your individual situation and needs. The grid breaks down the different factors involved in career change, allowing a better understanding and implementation of what at first appears to be a frightening shift.

We've also considered ways of upgrading skills and selling our talents to prospective hirers; how to understand what we do well, what we need to learn and how we can best represent ourselves in the marketplace. For some, the greatest work satisfaction can only be achieved by starting their own business. And statistics show that micro and small business sectors continue to increase, aided by new technologies which means a spare bedroom might easily become the hub of a multinational corporation. An ageing population and looming skills shortage means employers will finally have to taker older workers seriously and start offering them the flexibility, opportunities and training they want. But it's a two-way street and older workers will need to earn their place by remaining skilled, connected and energetic.

So how can you use this information to improve your own career path? Making career changes can feel threatening, as though we are letting go of a secure existence. The new 'rules of engagement' for today's workforce show there is no such thing as a secure job—in fact the statistics suggest the small business owner–manager has more security than the paid employee. Understanding this shift brings the realisation that security is gone, and this thought, although confronting at first, also frees us up to become more active in creating our own working futures. The only security possible is directly related to your willingness to take control of your own destiny. Now is the time for you to decide whether you wish to continue to perform your work on autopilot or whether you want to seize control and really start to zoom.

There are many reasons why you may not have made a wholehearted commitment to your work possibilities in the past—you may have been afraid of failing or succeeding (reaching above yourself), concerned about criticism from others, or your self-esteem may have been too low to allow you to believe you were worth the effort. What's past is past. Now is the time for you to decide whether you are living your own life, or tailoring it to suit someone else's expectations. If it's the latter, then you will need to be prepared to live with the results of this decision. If instead you are prepared to take full responsibility for your work future, and to commit to an ongoing program of change and review, then the following ten-point plan will help you synthesise the information you have read and take it forward:

1. let go
2. update yourself
3. invest in yourself
4. create your own business of one
5. take charge of your ongoing professional development
6. embrace technology
7. create and maintain peer networks
8. start a yearly career review
9. learn to love change
10. do it now

Let go

You cannot possibly move forward in any worthwhile endeavour unless you are prepared to farewell the folks, the first house, the old neighbourhood or old job. Until you turn the corner, you cannot embrace a new direction. Are you stuck at the crossroads, watching others move freely past? No one but you can make that first step which propels you forward. Take it. The next one will be easy by comparison.

Update yourself

A recent boom in 'reality' TV programs proves our appetite for life makeovers is endless. We seem to never tire of the story of the ugly duckling who grew into a beautiful swan. As 'unreal' as some of these makeovers are, the concept behind them is very sound. We cannot improve ourselves or take ourselves forward unless we are prepared to learn new ways of doing things. When applied to career planning, this means a willingness to find out what is really going on in the field of work we would like to do—which companies and individuals are doing a good job, and how they are doing this. Such an update requires effort. It can rarely be done in the workplace. Consider it the necessary homework to pass the exam of life. Staying current in your trade or profession is non-negotiable.

Now is the time for you to decide whether you wish to continue to perform your work on autopilot or whether you want to seize control and really start to zoom.

Invest in yourself

Becoming one of the best in your field takes a huge investment of both time and money. Malcolm Gladwell, author of *Outliers: The story of success*, suggests it takes at least 10,000 hours! The less money you have, the smarter and harder you will have to work to achieve your goals. Being willing to invest in yourself is a sure sign you are prepared to do the hard yards it takes to get the type of work you will enjoy the most. This investment may take the form of education or training, but it's also very much an attitudinal thing. The recent 'Best job in the world' campaign orchestrated by Tourism Queensland won more than $350 million of promotional coverage from a monetary investment of just $1.7 million. The intellectual investment was the critical difference—there were seven minds (two clients, five agencies) brainstorming the best way to highlight the delights of the islands of the Great Barrier Reef on a relatively low budget. Small budget, huge results. How much are *you* prepared to invest in your career prospects? And how can you maximise the return on this outlay?

Create your own business of one

The SWOT analysis of a business—identifying strengths, weaknesses opportunities and threats—had a good workout in Chapter 4. The point of viewing your work offering in this way is to encourage you to become very focused and professional in your understanding of your unique work DNA, to shore up those aspects which are weak, and to create a vibrant package which will be difficult for potential employers or hirers to resist. The 'job for life' passed away sometime in the last decade. Passive résumés and subservient interview techniques are not going to win the work you will love doing. You need to fully understand what it is you have to sell and market it passionately.

Take charge of your ongoing PD

As we have seen, very few companies are spending big dollars on training, particularly for those employees who are aged north of 50. Waiting for someone else to pay for or organise your ongoing professional development is not merely discouraging. It's a highly dangerous career strategy. As information becomes more readily accessible, largely due to technological change, so we need to be aware that every individual who is competing with us for work has access to this information and may be more prepared than we are to keep themselves vocationally relevant. Unless we seize the opportunity to keep learning about our profession we run the risk of slipping backwards—fast. As Commissioner Elizabeth Broderick so succinctly noted in Chapter 10, we all need to build resilience into our working lives and this is best done by taking a lifelong approach to learning, both formal and informal.

Embrace technology

Chapter 2 covered the rapid advance of new technologies and their impact on the way we do our work on a daily basis. It's difficult to understate this dramatic shift. More than half of the Chinese population are accessing the internet by mobile phone; a practice that probably seemed inconceivable just ten years ago, yet it is reality today. No one can predict how we will be using technology in ten years' time. What we can safely predict, however, is that those who refuse to at least consider incorporating new forms of technology into their work routines will be squeezed out of the workforce—sooner rather than later.

Create and maintain peer networks

While the workplace becomes evermore technologically sophisticated, the value of old-fashioned people contacts never becomes obsolete. The way we make and support these networks may change, with many professionals choosing to share news on social networking websites such as Facebook and LinkedIn, but peer support groups are just as important as they ever were. No matter how sophisticated online search and recruitment is becoming, it is word of mouth which often opens the door and secures the recommendation. Keeping in touch with colleagues both near and far is not just useful—it's how we learn, grow and have fun. As long as we remember to give back more than we receive.

Start a yearly career review

Career planning is no longer a 'set and forget' exercise performed when you leave school, college or university or suddenly find yourself out of work. It's a common observation that we will now have five or six or more careers in our lifetime, but we rarely connect that observation with the need for ongoing career reviews. Because we have traditionally undertaken this planning when we are under pressure (the need to get a new job has suddenly arisen) or under-skilled (why do we expect teenagers to have any idea of long-term career directions?) we think of the planning as a chore. It's not. It's a great opportunity to take a day or two away from our routine and really indulge our wildest dreams and hopes, pondering how they can fit with our current needs. The best time to conduct such a review is when we are relaxed, perhaps during the Christmas break. Circle a date on the calendar now, and make your career planning something you look forward to every year.

Learn to love change

We all know the only constant is change, yet so many of us seem to be surprised, if not alarmed, when change happens. Friends move away, neighbourhoods alter, children grow up, companies fail, jobs are lost. Daily newspapers are written because thousands of things have changed overnight, both locally and internationally. The only real choice we have when it comes to change is our attitude towards it. Are we going to resist innovation and cling to the old ways of doing things? Or are we going to make a determined effort to keep up-to-date with change and enjoy the way it can improve out lot? Perhaps we might even take Rupert Murdoch's advice and decide to 'get out in front of it'. The choice is yours.

Do it now

It's far better to wear out than rust, as the saying goes. Earlier on we considered the ingredients of a successful life; someone to love, something to do, something to look forward to. There is no substitute for personal relationships that are fulfilling, but meaningful work can and does offer some*thing* to love, something to do and something to look forward to.

Something to love might mean a cause, such as KOTO, founded by Jimmy Pham, which is indeed 'bigger than the self'. Something to do might be Les Bartlett building a community wood-fired oven, Natasha Boyd sharing books with school children, or Lisa Shergold sharing jokes with her older passengers who would otherwise be isolated. All these examples deliver the intense gratification described by Hugh Mackay as the reason we want to keep working. Getting out of bed and going to work becomes a privilege because we are doing something that really matters to ourselves and others. Something Trevor Barry thinks is worth far more than money.

It's uplifting to read about people who have created positive change in their own and others' lives. But it's even more satisfying to stop reading and start doing something more meaningful yourself. To create the type of work which is not just fun and engaging, but builds on the legacy you hope to leave for others.

What are you waiting for?

Your time starts now!

Notes and Resources

Introduction

The growing shortage of labour
Reinventing Retirement Asia Conference, jointly convened by AARP and
Government of Singapore, Singapore, 8–9 January 2009,
<www.aarpinternational.org/resourcelibrary/resourcelibrary_show.
htm?doc_id=887149>

Chapter 1   The world of work

Adapting to work change
Johnson, Dr Spencer, *Who Moved my Cheese?*, Random House, London, 1998
Salerno, Ann and Brock, Lillie, *The Change Cycle: How people can survive and
thrive in organizational change*, Berrett–Koehler Publishers, Inc. San Francisco,
2008, <www.ChangeCycle.com>

From money to meaning
Bridges, William, *Transitions: Making sense of life's changes*, Da Capo Press,
Cambridge, MA, 2004

Data on the death of full-time work
Australian Bureau of Statistics, 6361.0, *Employment Arrangements, Retirement and
Superannuation, Australia*, April to July 2007, 7 November 2008

'Project Hollywood'
Godin, Seth, *Tribes: We need you to lead us*, Piatkus, London, 2008

Increasing fragmentation of the day job

Matathia, Ira and Salzman, Maria, *Next: Trends for the future*, Pan Macmillan Australia Pty Ltd, Sydney, 1998

Richard Watson, *What's Next*, <www.nowandnext.com>

Chapter 2   Shift happens

Everything old is new again

Ross, Angus (ed.), *Selections from the* Tatler *and the* Spectator, Penguin Books, UK, 1982

The first electronic revolution

'Technological revolution leads political revolution', *Lateline*, ABC Television, 17 June 2009, <www.abc.net.au/lateline/content/2008/s2601256.htm>

Viewing the online world

Locke, Christopher, Levine, Rick, Searls, Doc and Weinberger, David, *The Cluetrain Manifesto*, 1999, published online at <www.cluetrain.com>

Future directions

Institute for the Future, *The Future of Work, Technology Foundations*, Palo Alto, California, 2007, <www.iftf.org/tech>

The amplified individual

Gorbis, Marina, *Organizational Change Coming Soon* for Roll Call News, Institute for the Future, 18 May 2009, <www.iftf.org/mgorbisorgchange>

Rupert Murdoch on new technologies

Murdoch, Rupert, *Who's Afraid of New Technology?*, Boyer Lectures, Lecture 2, ABC Radio National, 9 November 2008, <www.abc.net.au/rn/boyerlectures/stories/2008/2397933.htm>

Chapter 3   All about you

Locus of control

Rotter, Julian, *Generalized Expectancies for Internal versus External Control of Reinforcements*, Psychological Monographs, 80, Whole No. 609, 1966

Spector, P.E. 'Development of the Work Locus of Control Scale', *Journal of Occupational Psychology*, vol. 61(4), Dec. 1988, pp. 335–40

Zimbardo, Professor Philip G., <www.zimbardo.com/zimbardo.html>

Factors contributing to success

Nash, Laura and Stevenson, Howard, 'Success That Lasts', *Harvard Business Review*, 1 February 2004 <www.hbr.harvardbusiness.org/2004/02/success-that-lasts>

Gladwell, Malcolm, *Outliers: The story of success*, Little, Brown & Co., New York, 2008

Personality tests online

(note that some may require payment):
FiroB <www.cpp.com/products/firo-b/index.aspx>
John Holland <www.careerkey.org/asp/your_personality/take_test.html>
Myers-Briggs <www.myersbriggs.org>
Strong Interest Inventory <www.discoveryourpersonality.com/Strong.html>

The granddaddy of job search

Bolles, Richard Nelson, *What Color is Your Parachute?: A practical manual for job-hunters and career-changers*, Ten Speed Press, Berkeley, CA, 2003

Career-planning guides

Anderson, Maureen The Career Clinic: 8 Simple Rules for Finding Work You Love, AMACON books, American Management Association, New York, 2009

Cannon, Jan, *Now what do I do? The Woman's Guide to a New Career*, Capital Books Inc., Virginia, 2005

Farr, Michael and Shatkin, Laurence, *150 Best Jobs for Your Skills*, JIST Publishing Inc., Indianapolis, 2008

Harvard Business School, *Harvard Business Review on Managing Your Career*, Harvard Business School Press, Boston, 2002

Hustad, Megan, *How to be Useful: A Beginner's Guide to Not Hating Work*, Simon & Schuster UK Ltd., London, 2008

Good career-planning websites

The Riley Guide, a helpful US-based career portal offering career and employment information, <www.rileyguide.com>

Job Hunter, Richard Bolles' companion website to *What Color is Your Parachute?*, <www.jobhuntersbible.com>

Chapter 4   Your work DNA

Work interests and anchors

Butler, Dr Timothy and Waldroop, Dr James, 'Business Interest Index' in *Shaping Your Career*, Harvard Business Press, Boston, MA, 2008

Mueller, Sherry and Overmann, Mark, *Working World: Careers in International Education, Exchange and Development*, Georgetown University Press, Washington DC, 2008

Pocock, Dr Barbara, 'Australian Work and Life Index' (AWALI), *Work, Life and Workplace Flexibility 2009*, Pocock, Dr Barbara, Skinner, Natalie and Ichii, Reina, University of South Australia, <www.unisa.edu.au/hawkeinstitute/cwl>

Schein, Edgar H., *Career Anchors, Self Assessment,* 3rd Edition, Pfeiffer, A Wiley Imprint, San Francisco, CA, 2006, <www.careeranchorsonline.com/SCA/ESabout.do?open=es>

Chapter 5 What's out there?

Data on paid leave entitlements and contracts
Australian Bureau of Statistics, 6361.0, *Employment Arrangements, Retirement and Superannuation, Australia, April to July 2007,* 7 November 2008

The death of the 'organization man'
Pink, Daniel H., *Free Agent Nation: The future of working for yourself,* Business Plus, Hachette Book Group, New York, 2002

Finding meaning in our work
Bridges, William, *Transitions: Making sense of life's changes,* Da Capo Press, Cambridge, MA, 2004

Freedman, Marc, *Prime Time: How Baby Boomers will revolutionize retirement and transform America,* Public Affairs, Perseus Books Group, Cambridge, MA, 1999

Data on voluntary work
Australian Bureau of Statistics, 4441.0, *Voluntary Work Australia,* 2006

Volunteering
Volunteering Centre contact list:
National:
Volunteering Australia, <www.volunteeringaustralia.org>
Email: volaus@volunteeringaustralia.org
Tel: 03 9820 4100
ACT:
Volunteer ACT, <www.volunteeract.org.au>
Email: info@volunteeract.org.au
Tel: 02 6251 4060
NSW:
The Centre for Volunteering, <www.volunteering.com.au>
Email: info@volunteering.com.au
Tel: 02 9261 3600
SA & NT:
Volunteering SA & NT, <www.volunteeringsa.org.au>
Email: volsa@volunteeringsa.org.au
Tel: 08 8221 7177

TAS:
Volunteering Tasmania Inc., <www.volunteeringtas.org.au>
Email: <admin@volunteeringtas.org.au>
Tel: 03 6231 5550
QLD:
Volunteering Queensland, <www.volqld.org.au>
Email: vq@volqld.org.au
Tel: 07 3002 7600
VIC:
Volunteering Victoria, <www.volunteeringvictoria.org.au>
Email: info@volunteeringvictoria.org.au
Tel: 03 9642 5266
WA:
Volunteering WA, <www.volunteeringwa.org.au>
Email: info@volunteeringwa.org.au
Tel: 08 9482 4333
International:
Australian Volunteers International, <www.australianvolunteers.com>
International system of labour exchange, Willing Workers on Organic Farms
    <www.wwoof.com.au>

Working overseas
The Big Trip: Your ultimate guide to gap years and overseas adventures, Lonely
    Planet Publications Pty Ltd, Footscray, Australia, 2008

Federal Government (DEEWR) job guide
Job Guide, <www.jobguide.dest.gov.au/>

Table showing breakdown of Australian jobs sectors
Australian Government, Australian Jobs, 2008, <www.workplace.gov.au/
    workplace/Publications/ResearchStats/LabourMarketAnalysis/AustralianJobs/>

Fastest growing industry themes
New Age, 1965–2040, *IBISWorld*, 2009, data given to author

Chapter 6   Planning your next move

Grief in relation to work roles
Bridges, William, *Transitions: Making sense of life's changes*, Da Capo Press,
    Cambridge, MA, 2004

Career segues
Bolles, Richard Nelson, *What Color is Your Parachute?: A practical manual for job-hunters and career-changers*, Ten Speed Press, Berkeley, CA, 2003

Life coaches website
Find a Coach has a search engine to help you find a coach that matches your needs. <http://www.findacoach.net.au>

Chapter 7   Selling your talents

Data on finding work
Bolles, Mark Emery and Bolles, Richard Nelson, *Job Hunting Online*, 5th Edition, Ten Speed Press, Berkeley, CA, 2008

The gung-ho approach
Bolles, Richard Nelson, *What Color is Your Parachute?: A practical manual for job-hunters and career-changers*, Ten Speed Press, Berkeley, CA, 2003

The less-is-more approach
Corcodilos, Nick, *Ask the Headhunter*, Nicholas Brealey Publishing, London, 1997

The 'organic' approach
Ibarra, Herminia, *Working Identity: Unconventional strategies for reinventing your career*, Harvard Business School Press, Boston, MA, 2004

Vocational context
Job Guide example of search for events coordinator, <www.jobguide.thegoodguides.com.au/occupation/view/332311B>

Australian Jobs website
Labour market and vacancy reports including: Leading Indicator of Employment, Regional updates, Australian Jobs, Australian Regional Labour Markets, Job Outlook; Labour Economics Office; Skill Shortages; Small area labour markets; Vacancy Reports. <www.workplace.gov.au/workplace/Publications/ResearchStats/LabourMarketAnalysis>

'Living with the natives'
Corcodilos, Nick, *Ask the Headhunter*, Nicholas Brealey Publishing, London, 1997, p. 60

Sources of research for career interests
Smart Company <www.smartcompany.com.au>
Harvard Business Review website and magazine <www.hbr.harvardbusiness.org>

Tips on writing a killer resumé
McGraw Hill, *Resumes: Re-entering the job market*, McGraw Hill Professional
    Development, Columbus, OH, 2008

BTSO approach
Macfarlan Lane, <www.macfarlanlane.com.au>

Gary Henderson quoted in Pamela Oddy
'If you've got it, flaunt it', *YOURLifeChoices* magazine, Issue 33, January 2009

Technology subsidies
WorkVentures supply reconditioned computers from $250 for those on limited
    income, <www.workventures.com.au>
TadAust is a low charge Internet Service Provider (ISP) for those with a disability
    or on a pension, <www.tadaustconnect.org.au>
Making Ends Meet is a federal government program which offers a telephone and
    internet allowance, <http://tiny.cc/T4rvA>

Chapter 8   Skilling up

The sigmoid curve
Handy, Charles, *The Empty Raincoat: Making sense of the future*, Hutchinson,
    London, 1994, p. 48

Transferable skills
About.com career planning website offers a worksheet where you can rate your
    transferable skills: <http://careerplanning.about.com/od/careerchoicechan/a/
    transskillwksht.htm>
Bolles, Richard Nelson, *What Color is Your Parachute?: A practical manual for job-
    hunters and career-changers*, Ten Speed Press, Berkeley, CA, 2003
The notion of the three types of transferable skills was originally conceptualised
    by Alain Mounier in *The Three Logics of Skills*, Working Paper 66, ACIRRT,
    Sydney, 2001

Transferable skills checklist
The Australian Workplace website checklist: <http://www.workplace.gov.
    au/workplace/Individual/Jobseeker/Careers/CareerJobSearchTips/All/
    Usingourtransferableskills.htm>

People Skills

Carnegie, Dale, *How to Win Friends and Influence People*, Simon & Schuster, 1936, republished 1998

The STAR model

This can be found on the Australian Public Service Commission website, <www. apsc.gov.au/publications07/crackingthecodefactsheet5.htm>

Training more important than salary

CareerOne, *Hunting the (Hidden) Hunters: A new approach to activating Australia's latent job hunters*, February 2009, <http://www.careerone.com.au/c1/insite/report/hunting_the_hunters>

Yahoo!7 listing of trade magazines

Links to trade magazines by industry sector: <http://au.dir.yahoo.com/Regional/Countries/Australia/Business_and_Economy/Business_to_Business/News_and_Media/Magazines/Trade_Magazines>

Chapter 9   Be your own boss

Political and technological change create new opportunities for entrepreneurs

Craig Newmark quoting *The Cluetrain Manifesto* in Canfield, Jack, and Hendricks, Gay, *You've Got to Read this Book*, HarperCollins, New York, 2007

Data on Australian businesses, success rate and time in business

Australian Bureau of Statistics, 8175.0, *Counts of Australian Business Operators by Selected Characteristics*, 2007

Entrepreneur or technician?

Gerber, Michael E., *The E Myth Revisited: Why most small businesses don't work and what to do about it*, Harper Business, New York, 2001

Working hours for small business owners

Australian Bureau of Statistics, 6361.0, *Employment Arrangements, Retirement and Superannuation, Australia, April to July 2007*, 7 November 2008

Franchising

Franchising code of conduct, March 2008: <www.accc.gov.au/content/index.phtml/itemId/816482>

ACCC Franchise Manual and Guide to Franchising Code of Conduct: <www.accc. gov.au/content/index.phtml/itemId/816482 >
Franchise Council of Australia website: <www.franchise.org.au>

Business entry point downloadable guides
This website offers you simple and convenient access to all the government information, transactions and services you need to plan, start and run your business: <www.business.gov.au>
BEC Australia is a not-for-profit national network of Business Enterprise Centres. A great starting point for those wishing to create or purchase a business. <www.becaustralia.org.au>
New Enterprise Incentive Scheme (NEIS) is funded by the Department of Education, Employment and Workplace Relations (DEEWR). It helps those eligible to establish and run their own business. <www.neis.com.au>

Other useful resources
Berry, Tim and Parsons, Sabrina, *3 Weeks to Startup: A high-speed guide to starting a business*, Entrepreneur Press, Canada, 2008
English, John, *How to Organise and Operate a Small Business in Australia*, 10th edition, Allen & Unwin, Crows Nest, 2009
English, John and Moate, Babette, *Discovering New Business Opportunities*, Allen & Unwin, Crows Nest, 2009
Lessons Learned: Straight Talk from the World's Top Business Leaders—Managing your career, Harvard Business School Press Boston, MA, 2007, or online at <www.fiftylessons.com>

Chapter 10 New tricks

Bird, Caroline, *Second Careers: New ways to work after 50*, Little, Brown and Company, Canada, 1992
Bridges, William, *Transitions: Making sense of life's changes*, Da Capo, Cambridge, MA, New York, 1980
Erickson, Tamara, *Retire retirement: Career strategies for the boomer generation*, Harvard Business Press, Boston, MA, 2008
Stone, Marika and Howard, *Too Young to Retire: 101 Ways to Start the Rest of Your Life*, Plume, Penguin Group USA, New York, 2004
Stratford, David, *The Portfolio Years: The Happiest Days of Your Life: How to Create a Better Life in the Fifties And Beyond*, Information Australia, Melbourne, 2000

Older workers and retirement
Freedman, Marc, *Prime Time: How Baby Boomers will revolutionise retirement and transform America*, Public Affairs, New York, 1999

Research on Baby Boomers and retirement

Jackson, Natalie, Walter, Maggie and Felmingham, Bruce, *Australian Survey of Retirement Attitudes and Motivations (ASRAM)*, University of Tasmania, 2006 <www.ozretirementsurvey.com>

Demographic trends

Australian Institute of Health and Welfare <www.aihw.gov.au/mortality/life_ expectancy/trends.cfm>

Deficit model is outdated

Miller, Stanley, Abstract of a paper offered to Reinventing Retirement Asia: *Employment and Active Engagement beyond 50* conference, Singapore, 2009, <www.aarpinternational.org/resourcelibrary/resourcelibrary_show. htm?doc_id=887149>

Employment and active engagement beyond 50

Executive Summary: Reinventing Retirement Asia, *Employment and Active Engagement Beyond 50*, April 15, 2009 <www.aarpinternational.org/ resourcelibrary/resourcelibrary_show.htm?doc_id=887149>

The concept of 'generativity'

Vaillant, George, *Ageing Well*, Scribe Publications Pty Ltd, Carlton North, Melbourne, 2002

The four seasons of life

Bridges, William, *Transitions: Making sense of life's changes*, Da Capo Press, Cambridge, MA, 2004

The search for significance

Wasserman Davis, Kathryn, Projects for Peace <www.davisprojectsforpeace.org>

Data on age at retirement

Australian Bureau of Statistics, 4102.0, *Retirement and Retirement Intentions*, Australian Social Trends, 2009

Mythbusting list

Mythbusting, Business, Work and Ageing Centre for Research, Swinburne University <www.swinburne.edu.au/business/business-work-ageing>

Innovations in functions of manual labour
AARP International Employers Awards <www.aarp.org/money/work/articles/2009_
aarp_international_innovative_employers.html>

Baby Boomers' views on retirement
Dytchwald, Ken and Kadlec, Daniel, *With Purpose: Going from success to
significance in work and life*, HarperCollins, New York, 2009

Reynolds, Scott, Ridley, Neil and Van Horn, Carl, *A work-filled retirement: Workers
changing views on employment and leisure*, Rutgers University, Centre for
Workforce Development, August 2005

AgeWave research
Retirement at the Tipping Point, research by AgeWave conducted by Harris
Interactive, 2009 <www.agewave.com/RetirementTipping Point.pdf>

Miscellaneous resources

Harvard Business Review: On Managing Yourself, Harvard Business School Press
Boston, 2005

General change
Fallick, Kaye, *Get a New Life: How to Change the Way You Live*, Allen & Unwin,
Crows Nest, Australia, 2004

Salerno, Ann and Brock, Lillie, *The Change Cycle: How people can survive and
thrive in organizational change*, Berrett–Koehler Publishers, Inc. San Francisco,
2008 <www.ChangeCycle.com>

Business:
*Lessons Learned: Straight Talk from the World's Top Business Leaders—Managing
your career*, Harvard Business School Press, Boston, 2007, online at <www.
fiftylesssons.com/hbsp>

On unleashing your creative purpose
Cameron, Julia, *The Artist's Way: A Course in Discovering and Recovering Your
Creative Self*, Pan Macmillan Ltd, Oxford, 1995

——*Walking in this world: Practical strategies for creativity*, Rider Books, imprint of
Random House, London, 2002

An uplifting selection of useful self-development guides
Canfield, Jack and Hendricks, Gay, *You've Got to Read This Book*, Collins, imprint
of HarperCollins Publishers, New York, 2007

On building career confidence

Linder-Pelz, Dr Susie, *From Fear to courage: Managing Career Crisis*, Choice Books, Marrickville, NSW, 2002

General career search aide

Nemko, Marty, *Cool Careers for Dummies*, Wiley Publishing Inc., Indianapolis, 2007

Inspirational CDs on work, change and exploring our full potential

Whyte, David, *Crossing the Unknown Sea: Work as a Pilgrimage of Identity*, Riverhead Books, New York, 2001